The Garden Within

Reflections for Every Season of Life

Amanda E. Robinson

Copyright Page

The Garden Within
Reflections for Every Season of Life

Copyright © 2026 by Amanda E. Robinson
All rights reserved.

ISBN: 979-8-9945704-0-1

No part of this book may be reproduced, distributed, or transmitted in any form or by any means, including photocopying, recording, or other electronic or mechanical methods, without the prior written permission of the author, except in the case of brief quotations embodied in critical reviews and certain other noncommercial uses permitted by copyright law.

This book is intended for inspirational and reflective purposes only. It does not constitute medical, psychological, legal, or professional advice. The author assumes no responsibility for how the information in this book is used.

For Lexi, Brianna, and Josh
my living proof that love grows,
seasons change,
and anything is possible.

Remember who you are, beautiful soul.
You were never too much.
You were always meant to shine.
You are love,
you are light,
and you are here to bloom.

Author's Note

An Invitation Into the Garden

This book was not written to fix you.
It was written to walk with you.

The Garden Within is an invitation to notice the natural intelligence of your life — the way growth and rest, clarity and confusion, effort and ease all arrive in seasons. Just as nature does not rush its cycles, this book does not ask you to move faster than your own rhythm.

You do not need to read these pages in order.
You do not need to begin in Spring or finish in Winter.
You do not need to complete anything to be doing it "right."

Some days you may open to a single reflection and sit with it quietly. Other days you may move through several pages at once. Some seasons may resonate deeply, while others feel distant. All of that belongs.

This book honors the truth that life is not linear, it is cyclical. We return to the same themes again and again, each time with more awareness, more softness, more depth. You are not repeating yourself. You are deepening.

There will be moments in these pages that feel comforting. Others may feel clarifying. A few may feel tender. None of them are here to demand change. They are here to offer companionship as change unfolds naturally.

Think of this book as a garden path rather than a roadmap. You may linger where something feels alive. You may pass quickly through what does not speak to you right now. Nothing is wasted. Everything you need will meet you when you are ready.

Above all, remember this:
You are not behind.
You are not unfinished.
You are not broken.
You are living inside a season and seasons always turn.
May these pages help you listen more closely, rest more honestly, and remember what has always been growing quietly within you.

Welcome to the garden.

A Gentle Reading Map

Ways to Walk This Garden

There is no single way to move through The Garden Within.
This book is designed to meet you where you are, not where you think you should be.
You may read one page a day, as the reflections are written.
You may open to a season that matches your current inner landscape.
You may return to the same pages again and again as your life shifts.
Below are a few gentle ways to enter the garden. None of them are rules. All of them are invitations.

Walk With the Seasons

If you enjoy rhythm and continuity, you may choose to move through the book from beginning to end, allowing each reflection to unfold one day at a time. This approach mirrors the natural progression of seasons and supports gradual, layered growth.
Move slowly. Let each page have its own space.

Enter Where You Are

If you are in a season of growth, begin with Spring.
If you are expanding, expressing, or connecting, Summer may feel like home.
If you are reflecting, releasing, or simplifying, Autumn may speak to you.
If you are resting, surrendering, or renewing, Winter may welcome you.
There is no wrong season to begin. Nature does not ask where you've been before it responds

A Gentle Reading Map

Follow What Calls You

Some days, a word or theme will stand out. Trust that.
Open the book at random. Let a single reflection meet you.
Sit with it. Write if you wish.
Close the book when it feels complete.
This is not avoidance. It is intuitive listening.

Linger and Return

You may find yourself staying with one reflection for days.
You may skip ahead and later return to something you passed over.
This book is meant to be lived with, not finished.
The garden will still be here when you return.

Read Alone or Together

You may walk this garden privately, in quiet moments.
You may share reflections with a partner, friend, or group.
You may read aloud, journal, or simply sit in stillness.
Let the book adapt to your life, not the other way around.

A Final Reminder

There is nothing to complete here.
There is nothing to achieve.
This book does not measure progress. It honors presence.
Wherever you open these pages is the right place to begin.

About the Seasonal Embodiment Practices

How the body supports growth

Throughout this book, you will find Seasonal Embodiment practices, Simple, optional ways to involve the body in your reflection.

These practices are not exercises to perfect or techniques to master. They are gentle invitations to notice how the body participates in change.

What This Is

Each embodiment practice is a small, intentional physical action such as breathing, posture, or subtle movement designed to support the theme of the season you are in.

They are inspired by the understanding that the body often leads change before the mind fully understands it. When the body feels safe, open, or grounded, reflection deepens naturally.
You may think of these practices as ways to signal readiness to your nervous system rather than instructions to follow.

What This Does

The body and mind are not separate. How you breathe, sit, move, or rest influences how you think and feel.

These practices help by:

- Gently regulating the nervous system
- Supporting emotional safety and clarity
- Reinforcing the meaning of each season through physical experience
- Allowing insight to settle more deeply through repetition

Rather than pushing growth,
they create conditions where growth can occur organically.

You may notice:

- A sense of calm or presence
- Increased clarity or steadiness
- Easier access to reflection
- Subtle shifts in mood or energy

You may also notice nothing at all and that is perfectly fine. Change does not always announce itself.

How to Use Them

These practices are always optional.

You may:

- Try one once and move on
- Repeat the same practice across several days
- Skip them entirely
- Adapt them to suit your body

There is no correct duration, posture, or outcome.
Most practices take less than a minute.
If a practice feels uncomfortable, simply stop.
If it feels supportive, stay with it as long as you like.
You are encouraged to approach these practices with curiosity rather than discipline.

A Gentle Reminder

You are not required to do anything in order for this book to work.
The reflections stand on their own.
The embodiment practices are simply another doorway,
one that speaks directly to the body.
You may enter through thought, feeling, movement, or stillness.
All paths are valid.

Introduction

Welcome to the Garden!

Growth is often spoken about as something to chase, improve, or complete. But nature teaches us something different. It shows us that growth moves in cycles, quiet beginnings, full expression, thoughtful release, and necessary rest.

Nothing blooms all the time.
Nothing is wasted.
Nothing is rushed.

The Garden Within was created as a companion for that rhythm.
This book is not meant to fix you or push you forward. It is meant to walk beside you. Each page offers a moment of reflection, an invitation to notice where you are and to tend that place with care.

Like a garden, your inner world changes with time, experience, and season. Some days will feel light and open.
Others will feel heavy or still. All of them belong.

You may find yourself returning to certain pages again and again, while others quietly do their work in the background. There is no right way to move through this book.

Growth does not follow rules, it follows readiness.

Sometimes life feels like a cycle
you can't escape
patterns of self-sabotage,
lessons repeating
until you're weary.
Cycles are not prisons.
They end,
they evolve,
they transform.
Just as a flower drops its seeds,
every ending holds
the promise of beginning again

Seasons Of You

Spring

Awakening
5

Permission
15

Curiousity
25

Preparation
35

Intention
45

Trust
55

Patience
65

Fragility
75

Commitment
85

Adaptation
95

Confidence
105

Integration
115

Readiness
125

Summer

Presence
141

Energy
151

Expression
161

Connection
171

Joy
181

Essential Boundaries
191

Confidence In Presence
201

Play
211

Contribution
221

Discernment
231

Balance
241

Gratitude
251

Maturity
261

Fall

Awareness
277

Evaluation
287

Gratitude
297

Release
307

Simplifiction
317

Wisdom
327

Deliberate Boundaries
337

Responsibility
347

Integrity
357

Preservation
367

Distillation
377

Acceptance
387

Winter

Stillness
391

Rest
401

Incubation
411

Reflection
421

Acceptance
431

Surrender
441

Faith
451

Grace
461

Renewal
471

Hope
481

Emergence
491

Divine Essense
501

Completion
511

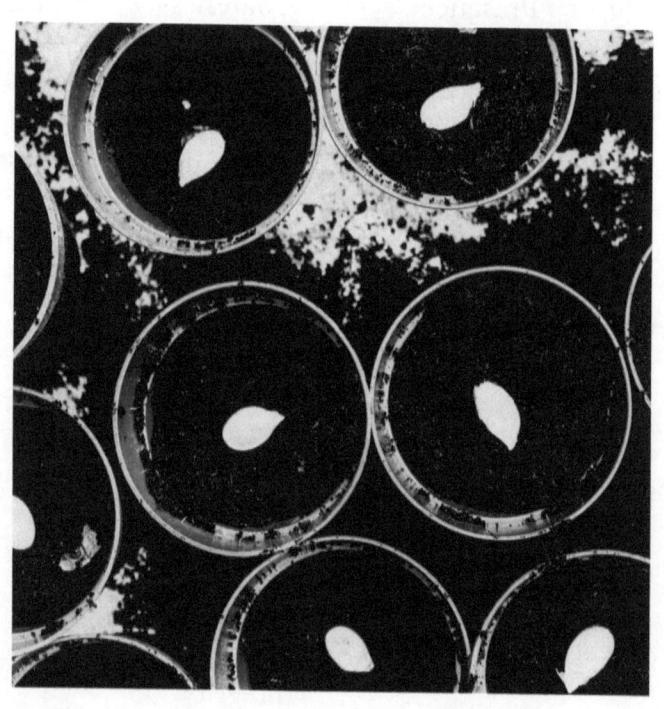

Spring

Emergence & Permission

"The Season of Beginning"

Spring is the season of emergence, the moment when life begins to move again after stillness. It is not sudden or forceful. It is quiet, tentative, and full of possibility. Spring reminds us that growth does not require certainty; it only requires willingness.

This season invites you to arrive gently, to listen for what is stirring within you, and to allow yourself to begin without needing to know where you are going. Spring teaches permission to take up space, to feel energy return, to explore curiosity, and to trust the first signs of readiness.

Throughout this season, you will explore themes of Awakening, permission, emergence, curiosity, trust, energy, choice, confidence, movement, expression, connection, play, and integration. Each theme offers a different doorway into beginning again.
Not from scratch, but from lived experience.

Spring does not ask you to rush forward.
It asks only that you notice
what is quietly waking.

Spring Ritual

Preparing the Ground

Spring is not the rush to grow, it is the quiet decision to begin.
Before seeds break the surface, the earth softens. It releases what has compacted and makes room for something new.
This ritual is an invitation to do the same.
You do not need special tools. You do not need certainty.
Only your attention.

Begin by finding a calm place, indoors or outside.
Sit comfortably. If it feels natural, place your feet on the floor or the earth.
Let your hands rest gently in your lap.
Take a slow breath in.
And an even slower breath out.

Bring your awareness inward and notice what feels tender, hopeful, or quietly ready within you. There is no need to name it perfectly. Growth often begins without language.
Now, imagine yourself tending a small patch of soil. You are not planting yet you are simply preparing. Clearing old debris. Loosening the ground. Creating space. With each breath, allow your body to soften as though it is becoming more receptive.

When you feel ready, gently acknowledge one intention for this season. Not a goal to achieve, but a quality you wish to cultivate such as patience, courage, openness, or trust. Hold it lightly. There is no need to force it into form.
Take one final breath.
And release the outcome.
Spring will do the rest.

Growth begins not with effort, but with willingness.
What you tend with care will grow in its own time.

The first signs of life stirring

Awakening

"Noticing what is quietly stirring within you."

Spring begins invisibly. Before anything breaks the surface, the earth responds to subtle shifts in light and warmth. Awakening within you follows the same rhythm. I t does not arrive fully formed. It arrives as a feeling, a question, a soft sense of readiness you cannot yet explain.

This moment asks only for attention. Not action. Not certainty. Just awareness. You may notice curiosity returning where there was once stillness, or a gentle discomfort where something no longer fits. These are signs of life moving again.

Awakening is not loud. It is intimate. It invites you to listen to what feels different now and to trust that noticing is enough for today.
Nothing needs to bloom yet.

Awareness is the beginning.

Awakening of Body

Reflection

Awakening often begins in the body
before the mind understands it.
A deeper breath. A softening in the chest.
A quiet release of tension you didn't know
you were carrying.
These small sensations are signs
that something is changing.
Today is not about interpreting them.
It is about noticing.
Your body is often the first place growth
announces itself.

Affirmation

I listen to the quiet signals of my body.
I honor what is gently awakening within me.

Reflection Question

Where in my body do I feel a subtle
sense of change or openness today?

Awakening of Emotion

Reflection

Emotional awakening rarely arrives as certainty.
It may show up as tenderness, hope, restlessness,
or a sense that something no longer fits the way it once did.
These feelings are not problems to solve, They are information.
Allowing them space without judgment gives them
room to clarify themselves.
What you feel today does not need to be permanent
to be meaningful.

Affirmation

I allow my emotions to inform me
without controlling me.

Reflection Question

What feeling feels most present for me right now?

Awakening of Choice

Reflection

Awakening deepens when you choose awareness.
This choice does not require action or change.
It simply asks you to stay present
with what is emerging rather than dismissing it.
Noticing is an act of respect toward yourself.
What you acknowledge gains permission to exist
and eventually, to grow.

Affirmation

I choose awareness over avoidance.
I honor what is asking to be seen.

Reflection Question

What am I choosing to notice today
that I might usually overlook?

Awakening of Rest

Reflection

Rest can feel counterintuitive
at the beginning of growth.
Yet awakening needs space.
Pausing allows sensations, emotions,
and insights to settle without being rushed into form.
Today invites you to rest from interpretation.
You are not required to make
sense of everything immediately.

Affirmation

I allow rest to support my becoming.
I do not rush clarity.

Reflection Question

Where can I give myself permission to pause today?

Awakening of Relationship

Reflection

As you awaken, your relationships may feel different
not because others have changed
but because you are more aware.
You may notice where connection feels nourishing
and where it feels distant.
This awareness is not meant to judge.
It simply invites honesty.
Growth often begins with noticing
how you experience connection.

Affirmation

I honor my experience within my relationships.
I allow awareness to guide connection.

Reflection Question

How do I feel most supported or seen right now?

Awakening of Perception

Reflection

Awakening shifts perception.
Familiar experiences may look different
when viewed through curiosity instead of habit.
Today offers an opportunity
to see your life with softer focus.
What happens when you release assumptions
and allow yourself to look again?

Affirmation

I allow my perception to evolve.
I see with openness and curiosity.

Reflection Question

What looks different to me today than it did before?

Awakening of Trust

Reflection

You may not yet know where this awakening leads.
That is not a failure, it is the nature of beginnings.
Trust grows when you allow what is stirring to exist
without demanding immediate direction.
Something within you knows how to unfold.
Your role is simply to stay present.

Affirmation

I trust the quiet beginnings within me.
I allow growth to reveal itself in time.

Reflection Question

What am I willing to trust without needing proof?

Awakening

Inviting the body to wake gently

Embodiment Focus

Gentle activation after rest
Nervous System Tone: Safety + readiness

Practice

- Begin seated or standing, wherever feels most comfortable

- Let your arms hang loosely by your sides

- Take a slow inhale through the nose and gently lift your shoulders

- Exhale through the mouth and let the shoulders drop

- Repeat this movement 3–5 times, slowly

After the final exhale, pause for a moment and notice any sensation of warmth, alertness, or subtle energy in the body.

Why This Supports Awakening

Spring awakening is not a jolt forward, it is a soft return to movement. This practice gently reintroduces motion and breath, signaling to the nervous system that it is safe to wake, stretch, and re-engage with life.

Awakening happens when the body feels invited, not pushed.

An opening allowed, not forced.

Permission

"Allowing yourself to begin without justification."

Spring offers permission simply by arriving. The earth does not ask whether it deserves to thaw, it responds to the call of renewal. In the same way, this season invites you to release the need for approval before you begin again.

Permission is an internal choice. It is the moment you stop waiting for the right conditions and allow yourself to take a first, gentle step. You do not need to explain your readiness or defend your desire to grow.

There may still be hesitation. That does not mean you are unready. It means you are human. Permission does not remove fear, it makes room for movement alongside it.

You are allowed to begin, exactly as you are

Permission of Body

Reflection

Permission often shows up in the body
before it becomes a conscious decision.
A sense of ease. A deeper breath.
A quiet softening when resistance loosens its grip.
Today invites you to notice where your body
already feels willing.
You do not need to convince yourself to begin
your body often signals readiness
long before your mind catches up.

Affirmation

I listen to my body's signals of readiness.
I allow ease to guide me forward.

Reflection Question

Where in my body do I feel a quiet sense of yes today?

Permission of Emotion

Reflection

Self-doubt often appears at the edge of new beginnings.
It is not a sign to stop,
it is a sign that you are standing somewhere unfamiliar.
Permission does not require confidence;
it requires honesty.
Today invites you to notice doubt
without letting it decide your direction.
Doubt can coexist with movement.

Affirmation

I allow myself to begin even when doubt is present.

Reflection Question

What would I allow myself to do if
doubt did not need to disappear first?

Permission of Choice

Reflection

Permission becomes real when it is chosen.
This choice does not need to be large or dramatic.
It can be as simple as acknowledging a desire
or taking one small step.
You do not need external approval
to choose your own beginning.
The decision to begin is yours to make.

Affirmation

I choose to honor my own readiness.
I allow myself to take the first step.

Reflection Question

What small choice could support my beginning today?

Permission of Rest

Reflection

Many people delay beginnings
because they feel the need to prove readiness.
Today invites you to rest from proving.
You do not need to earn permission
through exhaustion or certainty.
Rest allows you to begin from alignment
rather than pressure.

Affirmation

I release the need to prove my worth before beginning.

Reflection Question

Where can I stop proving and start allowing today?

Permission of Relationship

Reflection

Permission often brings change,
and change can shift relationships.
Today invites you to grant permission
not only to yourself,
but to others to be where they are,
to respond in their own time.
You are not responsible for managing
everyone's comfort with your growth.

Affirmation

I allow myself to grow without
managing others' reactions.

Reflection Question

Where might I be holding back
to keep others comfortable?

Permission of Perception

Reflection

When you grant yourself permission,
perception shifts.
You begin to see yourself as capable
rather than waiting.
Today invites you to notice how your self-image
changes when permission replaces hesitation.

Affirmation

I see myself as someone who is allowed to begin.

Reflection Question

How does it feel to view myself as ready enough?

Permission of Trust

Reflection

Readiness does not mean fear is absent.
It means something within you is willing.
Trusting your readiness is an act of self-respect.
Today invites you to honor that trust
even if the path ahead is not fully visible.

Affirmation

I trust my inner sense of readiness.
I allow my path to unfold naturally.

Reflection Question

What part of me already knows I am ready?

Permission

Allowing yourself to take up space

Embodiment Focus

Expansion with ease
Nervous System Tone: Safety + allowance

Practice

Stand with your feet hip-width apart, feeling the ground beneath you

As you inhale, gently open your arms outward, as if creating space around your body

As you exhale, soften the shoulders and let the arms relax

Move slowly and repeat 3–5 times, without forcing the breath

After the final exhale, pause and notice what it feels like to stand in your own space without apology.

Why This Supports Permission

Permission is not something the mind decides, it is something the body learns. This practice gently expands posture and breath, signaling to the nervous system that it is safe to take up space, to be seen, and to exist without contraction.

Permission grows when the body no longer feels the need to shrink.

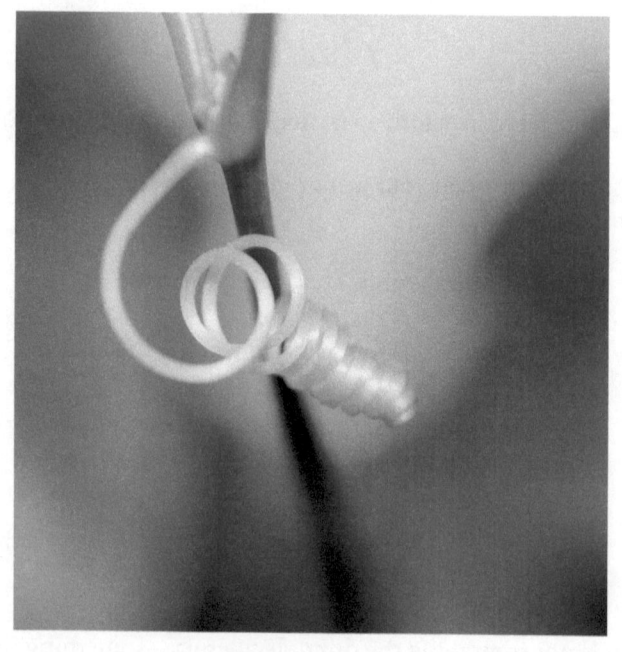

*Reaching toward what
is not yet known.*

Curiosity

"Exploring without pressure or expectation."

Spring does not demand certainty. It invites exploration. Curiosity is the energy of discovery without obligation. It's the willingness to look closer without needing answers.

In this season, curiosity may show up as questions, interests, or subtle pulls toward something new. You are not required to commit to everything you explore. Curiosity simply asks you to notice what draws you in and what no longer holds your attention.

When curiosity leads, growth feels lighter. Less forced. More alive. Let yourself wander a little. Let questions exist without resolution.

Curiosity opens doors that effort cannot.

Curiosity of Body

Reflection

Curiosity often begins as sensation
before it becomes thought.
A subtle pull.
A feeling of interest in the chest or belly.
Today invites you to notice
what your body leans toward naturally.
There is no need to justify the attraction.
Curiosity is simply information moving through you.

Affirmation

I listen to what my body is drawn toward.
I allow interest to guide me gently.

Reflection Question

What does my body feel curious about right now?

Curiosity of Emotion

Reflection

Curiosity carries emotion with it,
excitement, wonder, even uncertainty.
You do not need to resolve these feelings.
Allowing questions to exist without answers
creates emotional spaciousness.
Curiosity softens urgency and invites play.

Affirmation

I allow questions without demanding answers.

Reflection Question

What question am I allowing to remain open today?

Curiosity of Choice

Reflection

Curiosity becomes active when you choose
to explore rather than conclude.
Exploration does not require commitment.
It simply asks for openness.
Today invites you to choose exploration
over assumption, even in small ways.

Affirmation

I choose exploration over certainty.
I allow discovery to unfold.

Reflection Question

Where can I explore without needing a result?

Curiosity of Rest

Reflection

The need to know can be exhausting.
Curiosity invites rest from certainty.
Today offers permission to not know
and to let that be enough.
When you rest from answers,
insight often arrives quietly.

Affirmation

I rest in not knowing.
I allow understanding to emerge in its own time.

Reflection Question

What can I stop trying to figure out today?

Curiosity of Relationship

Reflection

Curiosity deepens connection
when it replaces assumption.
Today invites you to meet others with fresh interest,
noticing who they are now rather
than who you think they should be.
Curiosity creates space for authentic connection.

Affirmation

I meet others with openness and interest.

Reflection Question

How can curiosity soften a relationship today?

Curiosity of Perception

Reflection

Perception shifts when curiosity leads.
Labels loosen.
Stories soften.
Today invites you to look again at yourself,
at situations, at life with beginner's eyes.
What changes when you release fixed interpretations?

Affirmation

I allow my perception to stay open and flexible.

Reflection Question

What am I willing to see without labeling today?

Curiosity of Trust

Reflection

You may not know why curiosity
draws you somewhere.
Trust does not require explanation.
Today invites you to trust
that curiosity carries intelligence
even when the path is unclear.

Affirmation

I trust what I am drawn toward.
I allow curiosity to lead me forward.

Reflection Question

What am I willing to trust without
needing to understand why?

Curiosity

Inviting openness without urgency

Embodiment Focus
Gentle exploration
Nervous System Tone: Safety + openness

Practice

- Sit or stand comfortably, allowing your posture to remain relaxed

- Slowly turn your head to one side, letting your eyes follow the movement

- Pause briefly, noticing what comes into view

- Gently return to center and repeat on the other side

- Move slowly, with ease, for 3–5 rounds

After the final movement, return your gaze forward and notice any sense of spaciousness or interest in your surroundings.

Why This Supports Curiosity

Curiosity begins with the body's natural orienting response — the gentle turning toward something new. This practice invites exploration without demand, reminding the nervous system that it is safe to look, notice, and wonder.

Curiosity thrives when there is no pressure to act or decide.

The quiet work beneath the surface.

Preparation

"Tending the soil before planting."

Before growth takes hold, the ground must be cared for.
Old debris cleared. Space made. Preparation is the quiet, often
unseen work that supports what is to come.

In Spring, preparation may look like slowing down, setting
boundaries, or creating space, physically, emotionally,
or mentally.
It is not about productivity.
 It is about readiness.

You are not behind if you are preparing. You are honoring the
process. What you make room for now will shape what grows
later.

*The care you offer the soil
determines what can take root.*

Preparation of Body

Reflection

Preparation often begins with space.
In the body, this may look like releasing tension,
slowing your breath, or noticing where you
are holding more than you need.
Today invites you to soften where you can.
You are not clearing yourself out,
you are making room.
The body prepares for growth
by becoming more receptive.

Affirmation

I create space within my body for what is to come.

Reflection Question

Where can I soften or release tension today?

Preparation of Emotion

Reflection

Emotional preparation involves noticing
what lingers unnecessarily.
Old worries, unfinished thoughts,
or emotional residue can occupy space
meant for something new.
Today invites you to gently acknowledge
what is ready to be cleared.
Not through force, but through awareness.

Affirmation

I allow emotions to move through
me without holding on.

Reflection Question

What emotional weight feels ready to be released

Preparation of Choice

Reflection

Preparation is an act of discernment.
Choosing what matters creates space by definition.
Today invites you to make one small,
intentional choice that supports
what you wish to grow.
Preparation does not require many decisions,
just aligned ones.

Affirmation

I choose what supports my growth with care.

Reflection Question

What choice today creates more space
for what matters?

Preparation of Rest

Reflection

Rushing compresses space.
Preparation asks for patience.
Today invites you to rest from urgency
and allow readiness to form naturally.
You are not delaying growth, you are supporting it.

Affirmation

I release urgency and honor natural timing.

Reflection Question

Where can I slow down without consequence?

Preparation of Relationship

Reflection

Preparation also affects relationships.
This may look like clearer communication,
gentler boundaries, or making room for honesty.
Today invites you to consider how shared spaces,
emotional or physical can support mutual growth.

Affirmation

I prepare space for healthy connection.

Reflection Question

What would support greater ease
in my relationships right now?

Preparation of Perception

Reflection

Preparation sharpens perception.
You may begin to notice what feels cluttered,
outdated, or misaligned.
This awareness is not critical, it is caring.
Seeing clearly allows you to prepare wisely.

Affirmation

I see clearly what supports my growth.

Reflection Question

What am I noticing now that I hadn't seen before?

Preparation of Trust

Reflection

Preparation can feel invisible.
Trust reminds you that unseen work matters.
Today invites you to trust that what you are
tending now will support growth later,
even if results are not immediate.

Affirmation

I trust the quiet work I am doing.

Reflection Question

What unseen effort can I honor today?

Preparation

Creating readiness without urgency

Embodiment Focus

Grounded readiness
Nervous System Tone: Stability + gentle activation

Practice

- Stand or sit with both feet planted firmly on the ground

- Place one hand on your lower belly and one hand on your chest

- Take a slow inhale through the nose, feeling both hands rise slightly

- Exhale slowly through the mouth, allowing the body to settle downward

- Repeat 3–5 times, letting each breath feel steady and unforced

> After the final breath, pause and notice the sense of steadiness or quiet readiness in your body.

Why This Supports Preparation

Preparation is not about pushing ahead, it is about creating enough stability for what comes next. This practice grounds attention in the body and breath, signaling to the nervous system that it is safe to get ready without rushing or pressure.

True preparation feels like steadiness, not urgency

A choice gently placed.

Intention

"Choosing what you wish to nurture."

Spring brings many possibilities, but not all seeds are meant to be planted at once. Intention is the act of choosing with care.
It is not rigid planning.
It is gentle direction.

This season invites you to notice what you want to grow and why. Not from urgency, but from alignment. Intention asks you to be honest about where you want to place your energy.

You do not need to know the outcome. You only need to choose what feels worthy of your attention right now.

What you tend with intention grows with clarity

Intention of Body

Reflection

Intention often lives in the body
before it becomes a thought.
A sense of leaning forward.
A feeling of alignment when you imagine a certain path.
Today invites you to notice where your body
feels oriented toward growth.
You do not need to map the journey,
only to recognize the direction
your body already understands.

Affirmation

I listen to my body's sense of direction.
I honor what feels aligned.

Reflection Question

Where does my body feel naturally oriented right now?

Intention of Emotion

Reflection

Emotional clarity brings intention into focus.
What matters to you carries a distinct feeling
often quieter than urgency,
steadier than excitement.
Today invites you to notice which emotions
feel nourishing rather than draining.
Intention grows best when rooted
in what genuinely matters to you.

Affirmation

I allow my feelings to guide my intentions.

Reflection Question

What feeling do I want to nurture more of in my life?

Intention of Choice

Reflection

Intention is a choice made with care.
It does not require certainty or perfection.
Today invites you to choose one intention,
not as a demand, but as a direction.
Choosing gently allows intention
to remain flexible and alive.

Affirmation

I choose my intentions with kindness and clarity.

Reflection Question

What intention feels most supportive right now?

Intention of Rest

Reflection

Once intention is set, rest becomes essential.
You do not need to constantly reinforce
your intention through effort.
Today invites you to rest into alignment,
trusting that intention continues working
even when you pause.

Affirmation

I allow rest to support my intentions.

Reflection Question

Where can I rest without losing direction?

Intention of Relationship

Reflection

Your intentions influence how you show up with others.
Today invites you to notice what kind of presence
you want to bring into your relationships.
Intention here is not about control,
it is about choosing how you wish to participate.

Affirmation

I bring intention into my connections with care.

Reflection Question

How do I want to show up in
my relationships right now?

Intention of Perception

Reflection

Intention shapes perception.
When you know what you are nurturing,
your awareness naturally organizes around it.
Today invites you to notice how your attention shifts
when guided by purpose rather than habit.

Affirmation

I allow my perception to align with
what I am nurturing.

Reflection Question

What am I noticing more since setting intention?

Intention of Trust

Reflection

Once intention is chosen, trust carries it forward.
You do not need to revisit
or doubt your choice constantly.
Today invites you to trust that your intention
is enough to guide the next steps as they appear.

Affirmation

I trust the intentions I have set.
I allow them to unfold naturally.

Reflection Question

What would it feel like to trust my intention fully?

Intention

Setting direction with softness

Embodiment Focus

Clarity without force
Nervous System Tone: Grounded focus + ease

Practice

- Sit or stand comfortably, allowing the spine to be upright but relaxed
- Place one hand over your heart and one hand over your lower belly
- Take a slow inhale through the nose
- As you exhale, gently press your feet into the ground or your body into the chair
- After the exhale, pause briefly before the next breath
- Repeat 3–5 times, letting the breath remain natural

After the final breath, notice any sense of quiet direction or inner settling without needing to name it.

Why This Supports Intention

Intention is not something we push toward, it is something we align with. This practice brings attention to both the heart and the body's center, allowing intention to emerge as a felt sense rather than a mental demand.

When the body feels grounded, intention becomes clear on its own.

Roots growing unseen.

Trust

"Releasing control over how growth unfolds."

Once seeds are planted, the work changes. Trust becomes essential. You cannot pull growth from the soil by force. You must allow time, weather, and unseen processes to do their work.

Spring teaches trust through patience. There may be days where nothing seems to be happening. That does not mean nothing is happening.

Trust is not passive. It is the steady belief that growth continues even when progress is invisible.

Life grows best when it is allowed too.

Trust of Body

Reflection

Your body understands timing in ways
the mind cannot measure.
Muscles release when they are ready.
Breath deepens when it feels safe.
Growth follows similar rhythms.
Today invites you to trust your body's pace
instead of forcing it forward.
Nothing within you is late.

Affirmation

I trust my body's natural timing.
I allow growth to unfold gently.

Reflection Question

Where might my body be asking for patience today?

Trust of Emotion

Reflection

Trust does not eliminate uncertainty.
It coexists with it.
You may feel hopeful and unsure at the same time.
Today invites you to allow mixed emotions
without interpreting them as failure.
Trust grows when you stop
requiring emotional clarity
before moving forward.

Affirmation

I allow uncertainty without losing trust.

Reflection Question

What emotion can I allow without
needing to resolve it?

Trust of Choice

Reflection

Trust becomes active when you choose
to loosen control.
This does not mean disengaging,
It means allowing space for life to respond.
Today invites you to notice where you are gripping
too tightly and to practice easing your hold.

Affirmation

I choose to release what I cannot control.

Reflection Question

What can I gently let go of managing today?

Trust of Rest

Reflection

Forcing drains energy and narrows perception.
Trust restores both.
Today invites you to rest from pushing outcomes and allow yourself to be supported by the process itself.
Growth does not require constant effort.

Affirmation

I rest from forcing and allow ease.

Reflection Question

Where can I stop pushing and start allowing?

Trust of Relationship

Reflection

As you grow, relationships may shift naturally.
Trust invites you to allow these changes
without fear or control.
Some connections deepen, others soften.
Today invites you to trust that relationships
can evolve without being managed.

Affirmation

I trust relationships to grow and change naturally.

Reflection Question

Where can I release control in my connections?

Trust of Perception

Reflection

Trust changes how you perceive progress.
Instead of looking for evidence,
you begin to sense movement internally.
Today invites you to recognize growth
that cannot yet be measured.
Not all progress is visible.

Affirmation

I trust progress that I can feel, even if I cannot see it.

Reflection Question

What internal shift can I acknowledge today?

Trust of Trust

Reflection

At the heart of this movement is trust itself.
The willingness to allow what is becoming
to emerge in its own way.
You are not required to know the outcome.
Trust invites you to stay present with the unfolding.

Affirmation

I trust what is becoming within me.
I allow growth to take its time.

Reflection Question

What am I willing to trust
without needing certainty?

Trust
Allowing support

Embodiment Focus

Being held rather than holding
Nervous System Tone: Safety + reassurance

Practice

- Sit in a chair or lie down, allowing your body to be fully supported
- Gently lean your weight back into the surface beneath you
- Place one hand on your chest and one hand on your lower belly
- Take a slow inhale through the nose
- As you exhale, consciously allow more of your weight to sink into the support beneath you
- Repeat 3–5 times, letting the body soften a little more with each exhale

After the final breath, remain still for a moment and notice the sensation of being supported without effort.

Why This Supports Trust

Trust grows when the body experiences support without needing to stay alert or braced. This practice shifts the nervous system from self-holding into being held, reminding the body that it does not have to manage everything alone.

Trust is built when the body learns it is safe to rest into what already exists.

*Nourishment arriving
in its own time.*

Patience

"Honoring the pace of becoming."

Spring unfolds gradually. Buds do not rush open.
Roots deepen before stems rise. Patience is not delay,
it is alignment with natural timing.

You may feel eager for signs of progress. That eagerness is
understandable. But patience invites you to remain present
rather than future-focused.

What is becoming cannot be rushed without harm.
Let patience hold you steady as growth finds its rhythm.

Timing is part of wisdom.

Patience of Body

Reflection

Your body does not rush growth.
Healing, strength, and adaptation happen in rhythms
that cannot be hurried without consequence.
Today invites you to notice your natural pace
rather than pushing beyond it.
Patience in the body feels like cooperation
instead of resistance.
When you move with your body rather than against it,
growth feels safer and more sustainable.

Affirmation

I honor my body's natural pace.
I allow growth to unfold without pressure.

Reflection Question

Where can I slow down and move more gently today?

Patience of Emotion

Reflection

Emotions, like growth, need time.
Immediate clarity is not always available,
and that does not mean something is wrong.
Today invites you to allow feelings to develop
without rushing them into resolution.
Patience with emotion creates depth
and understanding.

Affirmation

I allow my emotions the time they need.

Reflection Question

What feeling am I allowing to unfold naturally?

Patience of Choice

Reflection

Patience is sometimes an active choice. Waiting can be a form of wisdom when action would come from urgency rather than clarity. Today invites you to notice where choosing to wait supports your growth more than pushing forward.

Affirmation

I choose timing over urgency.

Reflection Question

Where does waiting feel supportive right now?

Patience of Rest

Reflection

Patience deepens when you allow yourself to rest within the process instead of watching it anxiously. Today invites you to rest from monitoring progress. Trust that what is meant to grow is still growing even while you pause.

Affirmation

I rest within the process of becoming.

Reflection Question

Where can I stop checking and start resting today?

Patience of Relationship

Reflection

Patience extends beyond yourself.
Others grow at their own pace as well.
Today invites you to release expectations around
how quickly others should change or understand.
Patience in relationship creates space for authenticity.

Affirmation

I allow others their own timing.

Reflection Question

Where can patience soften my relationships?

Patience of Perception

Reflection

Patience changes perception.
You begin to notice subtle signs of progress
rather than waiting for dramatic shifts.
Small changes matter.
Today invites you to recognize growth
in the quiet places.

Affirmation

I notice growth in small, meaningful ways.

Reflection Question

What subtle sign of progress can I acknowledge today?

Patience of Trust

Reflection

Patience rests on trust.
Trust in timing, process, and life's intelligence.
Today invites you to trust that time
is working with you, not against you.
Nothing within you is stalled.
Everything unfolds when it is ready.

Affirmation

I trust the timing of my growth.
I allow time to support me.

Reflection Question

What would change if I trusted time completely?

Patience

Learning to stay with what is unfolding

Embodiment Focus

Settling into time
Nervous System Tone: Calm + regulation

Practice

- Sit comfortably with both feet on the ground
- Rest your hands loosely on your thighs or in your lap
- Take a slow inhale through the nose
- As you exhale, count silently to five, allowing the breath to lengthen naturally
- Pause gently at the bottom of the exhale before inhaling again
- Repeat 3–5 rounds, letting each breath feel unhurried

After the final breath, remain still for a moment and notice what it feels like to stay without moving toward the next thing.

Why This Supports Patience

Patience is not passive, it is the body's ability to remain present without rushing ahead. Lengthening the exhale calms the nervous system and signals safety, allowing the body to experience time as spacious rather than urgent.

Patience grows when the body learns there is no need to hurry the moment.

Tenderness that deserves care.

Fragility

"Protecting what is new and tender."

New growth is vulnerable. Early shoots can be damaged by frost, wind, or neglect. Fragility is not weakness, it is a stage of life that requires care.

Spring asks you to be mindful of what is tender within you. To protect it without hiding it. To honor its sensitivity without judging it.

Being gentle with yourself now is an act of strength. What is fragile today will not always be so.

Care creates resilience.

Fragility of Body

Reflection

New growth in the body often feels tender.
Muscles adjusting, energy recalibrating,
sensitivity increasing.
Today invites you to notice where your body
feels delicate rather than strong.
Fragility is not a flaw, it is a signal asking for care.
When you respond with gentleness,
resilience has room to form.

Affirmation

I treat my body with gentleness and respect.

Reflection Question

Where does my body feel tender
and in need of care today?

Fragility of Emotion

Reflection

Emotional sensitivity often increases
during periods of growth.
You may feel more affected by words,
moods, or memories.
This sensitivity is not weakness,
it is awareness expanding.
Today invites you to honor
your emotional tenderness without self-judgment.
What is sensitive is also alive.

Affirmation

I honor my emotional sensitivity as a sign of growth.

Reflection Question

What emotion feels especially tender right now?

Fragility of Choice

Reflection

Fragility asks for thoughtful choice.
Today invites you to choose actions that protect
what is new rather than expose it prematurely.
You are not hiding,
You are allowing time for strength to develop.
Gentle action is still action.

Affirmation

I choose actions that protect what is growing.

Reflection Question

What gentle choice supports my growth today?

Fragility of Rest

Reflection

New growth requires rest to stabilize.
Today invites you to rest the parts of yourself
that are still forming.
Overexposure can exhaust what is tender.
Rest is how fragility becomes resilience.

Affirmation

I allow rest to strengthen what is new.

Reflection Question

What part of me needs rest right now?

Fragility of Relationship

Reflection

As you grow, boundaries may still feel delicate.
Today invites you to protect new boundaries
without over-explaining or apologizing.
You are allowed to keep what is tender safe
while it gains strength.

Affirmation

I protect my boundaries with care.

Reflection Question

Where do I need to protect a boundary more gently?

Fragility of Perception

Reflection

Fragility is often misunderstood.
Today invites you to see tenderness
not as vulnerability to be hidden
but as growth in process.
Perception shapes how you treat what is new.
When you see fragility as strength forming,
your care becomes intentional.

Affirmation

I see tenderness as a stage of strength.

Reflection Question

How does my perspective change
when I honor fragility?

Fragility of Trust

Reflection

Trust in this stage means believing
that care is more valuable than speed.
What is nurtured slowly grows deeply.
Today invites you to trust that protecting
what is tender is not delaying your growth,
it is ensuring it.

Affirmation

I trust care to guide my growth.
I allow tenderness to mature naturally.

Reflection Question

What am I willing to protect rather than rush?

Fragility
Honoring tenderness without collapse

Embodiment Focus

Gentle containment
Nervous System Tone: Safety + protection

Practice

- Sit comfortably or lie down, choosing a position that feels supportive
- Gently wrap one arm around the opposite forearm, creating a loose self-hold
- Let the shoulders soften and the jaw relax
- Take a slow, quiet breath in through the nose
- As you exhale, lightly squeeze the arms together for a moment, then release
- Repeat 3–5 times, keeping the pressure soft and reassuring

After the final breath, allow your arms to rest naturally and notice any sense of warmth, steadiness, or quiet reassurance.

Why This Supports Fragility

Fragility does not need fixing — it needs protection. This practice introduces gentle containment through touch, signaling to the nervous system that tenderness can be held safely. The body learns that vulnerability does not mean exposure or harm.

*Fragility is not weakness.
It is life asking to be cared for.*

What holds growth steady.

Commitment

"Returning again and again with care."

Growth is not sustained by excitement alone. Commitment is what carries you forward when novelty fades. In Spring, commitment is gentle but consistent.

This is not about forcing yourself. It is about choosing to show up, even imperfectly. To tend what you've begun with steadiness rather than intensity.

Commitment honors your intention by meeting it repeatedly over time.

Small, faithful acts create lasting growth.

Commitment of Body

Reflection

The body builds strength through steady repetition,
not intensity.
Muscles adapt, rhythms establish,
and resilience forms when care is consistent.
Today invites you to notice what your body responds
to when you return gently, again and again.
Commitment in the body feels like familiarity
rather than strain.

Affirmation

I support my body through steady, caring attention.

Reflection Question

What gentle practice can I return to today?

Commitment of Emotion

Reflection

Commitment emotionally means staying present
even when feelings fluctuate.
Excitement may fade, doubt may rise, and interest may waver.
Today invites you to remain with your experience
without withdrawing.
Commitment does not require constant enthusiasm,
It requires honesty and presence.

Affirmation

I stay present with my emotions as they change.

Reflection Question

What feeling am I willing to stay with today?

Commitment of Choice

Reflection

Commitment becomes real
in moments of choice especially when
continuing feels ordinary or quiet.
Today invites you to choose to continue
without needing motivation or reward.
This choice strengthens trust in yourself.

Affirmation

I choose to continue, even when growth feels subtle.

Reflection Question

Where can I choose consistency over intensity today?

Commitment of Rest

Reflection

Commitment does not mean constant effort.
Rest is part of sustainability.
Today invites you to rest without stepping away entirely.
Remaining connected while resting
keeps momentum alive without depletion.

Affirmation

I allow rest to support my commitment.

Reflection Question

How can I rest without disconnecting today?

Commitment of Relationship

Reflection

Commitment in relationships looks like
presence, honesty, and follow-through.
Today invites you to notice
where consistency strengthens trust.
You do not need to overgive to be committed,
you only need to show up with care.

Affirmation

I show up in my relationships with steadiness.

Reflection Question

Where does consistent presence
matter most right now?

Commitment of Perception

Reflection

Commitment changes perception.
You begin to notice progress not in single moments,
but across time.
Today invites you to zoom out and recognize
how consistency shapes growth quietly and reliably.

Affirmation

I recognize progress that builds over time.

Reflection Question

What small change reflects my commitment?

Commitment of Trust

Reflection

Trust deepens when you see yourself
returning again and again.
Commitment builds confidence that you will
not abandon yourself when growth becomes quiet.
Today invites you to trust the power of steady presence.

Affirmation

I trust steady growth to carry me forward.
I remain committed with care.

Reflection Question

What does staying with myself look like right now?

Commitment

Choosing to stay present with what you've begun

Embodiment Focus

Steady grounding
Nervous System Tone: Stability + resolve

Practice

Stand with your feet hip-width apart, feeling equal weight through both feet

Gently press your feet into the ground, as if anchoring yourself in place

Take a slow inhale through the nose

As you exhale, softly engage your legs and core just enough to feel supported

Keep your gaze forward or slightly downward, steady and relaxed

Repeat 3–5 breaths, allowing the body to feel firm without tension

After the final breath, pause and notice the sensation of being rooted, present, supported, and still choosing to stand where you are.

Why This Supports Commitment

Commitment is not about force or endurance; it is about staying connected to the ground beneath you. This practice reinforces a felt sense of stability and choice, reminding the nervous system that commitment can be calm, embodied, and self-supporting.

Commitment grows when the body feels steady enough to remain.

Finding a new way forward.

Adaptation

"Responding to change with flexibility."

Spring weather shifts constantly. Warm days give way to cold nights. Growth adjusts accordingly. Adaptation is the ability to respond rather than resist.

You may need to change your approach as you go. That does not mean you failed. It means you are paying attention.

Flexibility allows growth to continue even when conditions change.

Adaptation is intelligence in motion

Adaptation of Body

Reflection

The body is designed to adapt.
It shifts posture, redistributes energy,
and responds to new demands
without needing conscious instruction.
Today invites you to notice how your body
naturally adjusts when something changes.
Adaptation in the body is not resistance,
It is intelligence at work.

Affirmation

I allow my body to adjust naturally.
I move with change rather than against it.

Reflection Question

How is my body responding to change right now?

Adaptation of Emotion

Reflection

Change often brings mixed emotions:
Anticipation, discomfort, curiosity, grief.
Emotional adaptation means allowing these feelings
to coexist without needing to choose one.
Today invites you to let emotions move freely
rather than locking into a single response.

Affirmation

I allow my emotions to adapt as needed.

Reflection Question

What emotion am I allowing to shift today?

Adaptation of Choice

Reflection

Adaptation becomes conscious when you
choose to adjust rather than insist.
This does not mean giving up,
it means responding wisely.
Today invites you to notice where a small adjustment
could bring more ease or alignment.

Affirmation

I choose flexibility without losing direction.

Reflection Question

Where can I make a small adjustment today?

Adaptation of Rest

Reflection

Change can be tiring,
even when it is positive.
Today invites you to rest without disengaging.
Rest allows adaptation to integrate
rather than overwhelm.
You do not need to rush your adjustment.

Affirmation

I allow rest to support my adaptation.

Reflection Question

Where do I need to rest while adjusting?

Adaptation of Relationship

Reflection

As you change,
relationships may require new ways of relating.
Today invites you to notice where
flexibility creates connection rather than distance.
Adaptation in relationship is an act of care
for yourself and others.

Affirmation

I adapt with openness in my relationships.

Reflection Question

Where can flexibility support connection today?

Adaptation of Perception

Reflection

Adaptation shifts perception.
Change no longer feels like disruption,
it becomes information.
Today invites you to view change as guidance
rather than obstacle.
What is adjusting may be supporting your growth.

Affirmation

I see change as a source of guidance.

Reflection Question

How might change be supporting me right now?

Adaptation of Trust

Reflection

Trust grows when you allow yourself to adjust without self-judgment.
You are not inconsistent. You are responsive.
Today invites you to trust that adaptation strengthens rather than weakens your path.

Affirmation

I trust my ability to adapt.
I allow flexibility to support my growth.

Reflection Question

What adjustment can I trust today?

Adaptation
Responding with flexibility

Embodiment Focus

Fluid adjustment
Nervous System Tone: Safety + responsiveness

Practice

Stand with your feet hip-width apart, knees softly bent

Slowly shift your weight to one foot, noticing the change

Pause briefly, then gently shift your weight to the other foot

Allow the movement to be small and unhurried

Let your arms move naturally if they wish

Continue shifting side to side for 30–60 seconds, breathing comfortably

After the movement, return to stillness and notice any sense of ease, balance, or adaptability in the body.

Why This Supports Adaptation

Adaptation is the body's ability to respond without panic or rigidity. Gentle weight shifting teaches the nervous system that change can be met gradually and safely. The body learns that adjustment does not require abandoning stability — it simply asks for responsiveness.

Adaptation grows when movement remains soft and choice-based.

Expansion without apology.

Confidence

"Standing with what is growing."

As growth becomes more visible, confidence begins to form. Not bravado, but quiet assurance. Confidence grows when you acknowledge what is taking shape.

Spring confidence does not demand certainty. It simply stands beside what is becoming without diminishing it.

Let yourself recognize progress without rushing ahead.

Confidence begins with acknowledgment.

Confidence of Body

Reflection

Confidence often shows up in the body
before it becomes a thought.
A steadier stance.
A relaxed breath.
Less bracing against what might happen next.
Today invites you to notice how your body
carries itself when it feels supported.
This is not force, It is stability forming.

Affirmation

I trust the strength growing within my body.

Reflection Question

Where do I feel more grounded or steady than before?

Confidence of Emotion

Reflection

Emotional confidence is subtle.
It does not shout certainty,
It whispers trust.
You may notice less self-questioning,
or a softer response to doubt.
Today invites you to let belief in yourself form naturally,
without demanding proof.

Affirmation

I allow confidence to grow quietly within me.

Reflection Question

What feels more settled or assured
emotionally right now?

Confidence of Choice

Reflection

Confidence grows when you choose
yourself in small, consistent ways.
Today invites you to notice where you are already
supporting your growth, perhaps without realizing it.
Choosing self-support reinforces trust
in your ability to move forward.

Affirmation

I choose to support myself with care.

Reflection Question

What choice today reflects trust in myself?

Confidence of Rest

Reflection

Confidence deepens when you allow yourself
to rest in what is already working.
You do not need to constantly improve or adjust.
Today invites you to pause and acknowledge stability without
rushing to the next step.

Affirmation

I allow myself to rest in what is working.

Reflection Question

Where can I stop fixing and start appreciating?

Confidence of Relationship

Reflection

Confidence in relationship looks like authenticity. You may find yourself speaking more honestly or holding boundaries with less explanation. Today invites you to show up as you are, trusting that authenticity strengthens connection.

Affirmation

I show up as myself with confidence.

Reflection Question

Where can I be more authentic today?

Confidence of Perception

Reflection

Confidence shifts perception.
You begin to notice progress instead of gaps.
Today invites you to see what has grown
without minimizing it.
Recognition strengthens what is already forming.

Affirmation

I see and acknowledge my growth.

Reflection Question

What progress can I recognize today?

Confidence of Trust

Reflection

At its core, confidence is trust in your presence.
You do not need to be more prepared
or perfected to stand where you are.
Today invites you to trust that
who you are right now is enough to continue.

Affirmation

I trust my presence and my path.
I stand with what is growing.

Reflection Question

What would it feel like to trust myself
fully in this moment?

Confidence

Standing in yourself without effort

Embodiment Focus

Grounded presence
Nervous System Tone: Safety + embodied assurance

Practice

Stand with your feet hip-width apart, knees softly unlocked

Gently lengthen through the spine, as if being lifted from the crown of the head

Let your shoulders roll back slightly and then soften down

Take a slow inhale through the nose

As you exhale, allow your chest to remain open without tension

Let your gaze rest forward at eye level, soft and steady

Breathe here for 3–5 slow breaths, without forcing posture

After the final breath, notice how it feels to stand upright, open, and at ease in your own body.

Why This Supports Confidence

Confidence is communicated through posture and presence long before it becomes a thought. This practice aligns the body into an open, balanced stance while signaling safety to the nervous
system. The body learns that confidence can be calm, grounded, and natural, not something that must be summoned or performed.

Confidence grows when the body feels at home in itself.

Many parts becoming one.

Integration

"Noticing how far you've come."

Before Spring turns outward toward expansion, there is a moment of reflection. Integration invites you to notice what has changed, even subtly.

You may not feel transformed, but you are not the same. Growth often reveals itself in perspective rather than results.

Take this moment to acknowledge the work you've done, the patience you've practiced, and the trust you've learned.

Integration allows growth to settle.

Integration of Body

Reflection

Your body holds memory.
Not just of strain or injury,
but of growth, adaptation, and learning.
Today invites you to notice how your body
feels different than it once did:
perhaps steadier, more open, or less guarded.
Integration happens when the body
no longer needs reminders. It simply knows.

Affirmation

My body integrates growth naturally and wisely.

Reflection Question

What feels different in my body compared to before?

Integration of Emotion

Reflection

As growth integrates, emotions often soften.
What once felt intense may now feel manageable.
What once felt confusing may now feel familiar.
Today invites you to notice emotional shifts
without analyzing them.
Integration does not require explanation,
it reveals itself through ease.

Affirmation

I allow my emotions to settle into understanding.

Reflection Question

What emotion feels more settled than it used to?

Integration of Choice

Reflection

Integration requires acknowledgment.
Today invites you to consciously recognize
the changes you've made, small or large.
Choosing to acknowledge progress helps it take root.
What you honor becomes part of you.

Affirmation

I choose to recognize my progress.

Reflection Question

What change am I willing to acknowledge today?

Integration of Rest

Reflection

Integration deepens when you rest within it.
You do not need to build immediately
upon what you've learned.
Today invites you to pause and allow change to settle.
Rest allows growth to become stable.

Affirmation

I allow rest to support integration.

Reflection Question

Where can I pause and let change settle?

Integration of Relationship

Reflection

Growth becomes real in relationship.
You may notice yourself responding differently,
communicating more clearly,
or holding space with greater ease.
Today invites you to observe how integration shows up
in connection without judgment.

Affirmation

I integrate growth through my relationships.

Reflection Question

How have my interactions shifted recently?

Integration of Perception

Reflection

Integration shifts self-perception.
You may see yourself as more capable,
more grounded, or more whole.
Today invites you to notice how your view
of yourself has changed.
Perception is often the clearest sign of growth.

Affirmation

I see myself with clarity and compassion.

Reflection Question

How has my perception of myself evolved?

Integration of Trust

Reflection

Integration completes when trust forms.
Trust in what you've learned.
Trust in how you've changed.
You do not need to revisit every lesson.
Today invites you to trust that growth has taken hold.

Affirmation

I trust what I have integrated.
I carry my growth forward with confidence.

Reflection Question

What learning am I ready to trust fully now?

Integration

Allowing what has emerged to settle into wholeness

Embodiment Focus

Whole-body coherence
Nervous System Tone: Safety + completion

Practice

Sit or stand comfortably, allowing your body to choose a natural posture

Place one hand on your heart and one hand on your lower belly

Take a slow inhale through the nose, sensing the body as a whole

As you exhale, gently scan from head to feet, noticing areas of warmth, ease, or neutrality

Allow the breath to move naturally without directing it

Repeat 3–5 breaths, letting awareness soften rather than concentrate

After the final breath, rest for a moment in stillness and notice the feeling of being gathered, nothing needing to move, fix, or change.

Why This Supports Integration

Integration is the body's ability to hold many experiences without fragmentation. This practice invites awareness to include the whole body at once, signaling completion and safety to the nervous system. The body learns that growth does not need to remain active to be real, it can settle, belong, and become part of you.

Integration happens when nothing is excluded.

*Fully formed,
waiting for the moment.*

Readiness

"Preparing to step into expansion."

As Spring draws to a close, readiness emerges naturally.
Not urgency, readiness.
The sense that what you've been tending is prepared for more light.

You do not need to push forward. Expansion will arrive on its own time. Readiness is simply the recognition that you are no longer at the beginning.

Something within you is stronger now.

Growth knows when it is time to rise.

Readiness of Body

Reflection

Readiness often arrives as
a sense of capability in the body.
You may feel more stable, more energized,
or simply less hesitant.
Today invites you to notice how your body
signals preparedness, not through tension,
but through ease.
You do not need to push forward.
Readiness is already present.

Affirmation

My body holds the strength it needs.
I trust its readiness.

Reflection Question

Where do I feel more capable or steady than before?

Readiness of Emotion

Reflection

As readiness forms,
emotions often feel more spacious.
There may be less fear around what comes next
and more openness to possibility.
Today invites you to notice emotional availability:
not excitement or certainty, but willingness.
Willingness is often the truest sign of readiness.

Affirmation

I am emotionally open to what comes next.

Reflection Question

What emotion feels more open or available now?

Readiness of Choice

Reflection

Readiness becomes real
when you choose to step forward:
not dramatically, but intentionally.
Today invites you to notice where a small forward choice
feels natural rather than forced.
You are not leaping.
You are moving when the ground
feels solid beneath you.

Affirmation

I choose forward movement with ease.

Reflection Question

What small step feels ready to be taken?

Readiness of Rest

Reflection

Just before expansion,
rest becomes especially important.
Today invites you to pause:
not as hesitation, but as preparation.
Rest gathers energy and steadies intention.
Expansion supported by rest is sustainable.

Affirmation

I allow rest to prepare me for what's next.

Reflection Question

Where can I pause before moving forward?

Readiness of Relationship

Reflection

Readiness shows up in how you relate.
You may feel more comfortable being seen,
clearer in your boundaries,
or more open to connection.
Today invites you to notice relational readiness
not as perfection, but as presence.

Affirmation

I meet others from a place of readiness.

Reflection Question

How does readiness show up in my relationships?

Readiness of Perception

Reflection

Perception shifts as readiness emerges.
The path ahead may not be fully visible,
but it feels less intimidating.
Today invites you to notice how
your view of the future has softened.
You do not need a map, only a sense of direction.

Affirmation

I see the path ahead with calm openness.

Reflection Question

How has my perception of what's next changed?

Readiness of Trust

Reflection

The final act of readiness is trust,
trust in yourself, trust in timing,
trust in the cycle turning naturally.
Today invites you to honor the work
you've done in this season.
You are not beginning from nothing.
You are carrying strength forward.

Affirmation

I trust myself as I enter what comes next.
I am ready for expansion.

Reflection Question

What does trusting this transition
feel like in my body?

Readiness

Standing open to what may arrive

Embodiment Focus

Available presence
Nervous System Tone: Stability + gentle anticipation

Practice

- Stand with your feet hip-width apart, weight evenly distributed

- Let your arms rest naturally by your sides

- Take a slow inhale through the nose

- As you exhale, subtly lean your weight forward just a fraction not enough to move, only enough to sense direction

- Pause briefly, then gently return to neutral

- Repeat this micro-shift 3–5 times, moving slowly and with awareness

After the final repetition, stand still and notice the feeling of being poised, grounded, yet open to motion.

Why This Supports Readiness

Readiness lives in the space between stillness and movement. This practice introduces the body to forward orientation without forcing action, teaching the nervous system that it is safe to be available without needing to decide or act yet.

Readiness is not rushing ahead.
It is knowing you could move and
trusting the moment to tell you when.

Crossing the Threshold

From Spring into Summer

Reflection

What Has Begun

Spring asks for courage, The courage to begin without certainty. It invites curiosity, tenderness, and the willingness to tend what is new.

Over this season, something has stirred. Perhaps quietly. Perhaps unevenly. Growth rarely follows a straight line. Some days felt hopeful, others uncertain. All of them mattered.

As Spring gives way to Summer, the work shifts. What was once fragile now seeks light. What was planted asks not just for care, but for presence. This moment is not about rushing forward. It is about noticing what has taken root and deciding how you wish to stand beside it.

Before moving on, pause here. Honor what you showed up for. Acknowledge what changed within you, even if no one else can see it yet. Integration is part of growth. Nothing needs to be perfected before you continue.

Summer will invite more visibility, energy, and expression. First let yourself witness what has already begun.

Crossing the Threshold

Guided Reflection Questions

Take your time with these.
Answer what feels right. Leave the rest.

- What did this Spring awaken in me?
- What felt most nourishing to tend?
- What challenged me as I began again?
- Where did I practice patience instead of force?
- What am I proud of showing up for?
- What am I ready to carry forward into the next season?

Preparing for Expansion

One word that describes my Spring

One quality I want to strengthen in Summer

One thing I am ready to release before moving forward

*Leave space here.
Growth continues even in stillness.*

Summer

Expression & Expansion

The Season of Aliveness

Summer is the season of aliveness when what has quietly emerged is ready to be lived, expressed, and shared. Energy turns outward. Movement becomes more natural. Life asks not just to be felt, but to be engaged.

This season invites you to inhabit your presence fully to let your voice, your joy, your creativity, and your connection move into the world. Summer is not about striving or proving. It is about learning how to stay open and alive without losing yourself in the process.

Summer teaches balance through experience. It shows us how to hold joy without excess, confidence without performance, and connection without depletion. It asks us to explore boundaries not as limits, but as containers that allow energy to flow sustainably.

Throughout this season, you will explore themes of presence, energy, expression, connection, joy, essential boundaries, confidence in presence, play, contribution, discernment, balance, gratitude, and maturity. Each theme offers a way to practice being fully alive while remaining grounded and whole.

Summer does not ask you to give more than you have.
It asks you to live from what is already full.

Summer Ritual

Standing in the Light

Summer is the season of presence. What has taken root now reaches upward, not to prove itself, but to meet the light that is already available. This ritual invites you to step fully into where you are without shrinking, rushing, or holding back.

Begin by standing or sitting upright in a space where you feel comfortable. If possible, let your feet connect with the floor or the ground beneath you. Allow your spine to lengthen naturally, as though you are giving yourself permission to take up space.

Take a slow breath in through your nose.
Let it travel all the way down into your body.
Exhale gently through your mouth.

Bring your awareness to your body. Notice where you feel open and where you feel guarded. There is no need to change anything. Summer does not ask for perfection—it asks for honesty.

Now imagine warmth surrounding you. It may feel like sunlight on your skin or simply a sense of openness in your chest. Let this warmth reach the parts of you that are ready to be seen. Not all at once. Only as much as feels safe.
Quietly acknowledge one truth about yourself that feels alive right now. This is not something to announce or defend. It is something to stand beside with confidence.

Take one final breath.
And allow yourself to remain visible to yourself.

You do not need to grow louder to be radiant.
Presence is enough.

Fully here, fully felt.

Presence

"Fully inhabiting where you are."

Summer invites you into the moment. Light lingers longer, days feel fuller, and life asks to be lived where it is happening now.

Presence is the practice of arriving in body, breath, and attention without reaching ahead or pulling away.
In this season, presence is grounding. It steadies the intensity of expansion by anchoring you in what is real and available.

You are not asked to do more. You are asked to be here.
When you are present, growth feels less like striving and more like participation.

This moment is enough to stand in.

Presence of Body

Reflection

Presence begins in the body.
In Summer, the body invites you to arrive fully,
to feel your feet on the ground,
the air on your skin, the rhythm of your breath.
Today is not about effort or improvement.
It is about inhabiting yourself as you are.
When you arrive in your body, life meets you there.

Affirmation

I arrive fully in my body and this moment.

Reflection Question

What helps me feel most present
in my body right now?

Presence of Emotion

Reflection

Summer brings heightened emotion
like joy, intensity, tenderness, desire.
Presence invites you to feel what is alive
without editing it.
Today asks only that you notice
your emotional landscape as it is.
You do not need to manage or resolve
what you feel to be present with it.

Affirmation

I allow myself to feel what is alive within me.

Reflection Question

What emotion feels most alive right now?

Presence of Choice

Reflection

Presence is a choice to stay, especially when distraction is easier.
Today invites you to choose this moment rather than rushing to the next.
Staying does not mean stagnation.
It means participation.
When you stay, life becomes more vivid.

Affirmation

I choose to stay present with what is here.

Reflection Question

Where can I choose to stay instead of rushing ahead?

Presence of Rest

Reflection

Rest can be an act of presence.
Today invites you to rest without leaving the moment.
To allow stillness to deepen awareness
rather than escape it.
Presence does not require constant engagement.
Sometimes it is simply being.

Affirmation

I rest while remaining present.

Reflection Question

How can I rest without checking out today?

Presencee of Relationship

Reflection

Presence transforms connection.
When you listen fully, speak honestly, and respond
without rehearsal, relationships feel more alive.
Today invites you to offer presence as a form of care.
You do not need to fix or perform, only to just be here.

Affirmation

I offer my presence freely and sincerely.

Reflection Question

How does presence change the way
I connect with others?

Presence of Perception

Reflection

Presence sharpens perception.
Colors seem brighter. Details emerge.
Today invites you to see what is actually here
rather than what you expect or assume.
When perception clears, appreciation often follows.

Affirmation

I see clearly what is here now.

Reflection Question

What do I notice when I slow down and really look?

Presence Of Trust

Reflection

Presence requires trust.
Trust that this moment is enough to stand in.
You do not need to rush toward meaning or outcome.
Today invites you to trust that being here
is already participating fully in life.

Affirmation

I trust the value of this moment.
I allow presence to be enough.

Reflection Question

What changes when I trust this moment fully?

Presence

Staying Here While in Motion

Embodiment Focus

Awareness during activity
Nervous System Tone: Regulation + engagement

Practice

- Stand comfortably and begin a slow, natural sway side to side

- Let your arms move freely with the motion

- As you sway, bring attention to the soles of your feet

- Take 3–5 natural breaths, staying aware of both movement and grounding

After the movement, pause and notice how presence can remain even while the body is active.

Why This Supports Presence

Summer presence is not stillness.
It is awareness carried into motion.

This practice trains the nervous system to stay regulated while moving, reminding the body that aliveness and presence can coexist.

You can be here, even while you move.

Life moving with purpose.

Energy

"Working with vitality rather than against it."

Summer brings an abundance of energy, but energy is not limitless. It rises, falls, and responds to how it is used. This theme invites you to notice your vitality where it flows easily and where it drains away.

You are not meant to be constantly active. Energy is sustained through rhythm, not pressure. Learning to listen to your body's signals allows you to expand without depletion.

When you honor energy, it becomes a source of support rather than demand.

Vitality thrives when it is respected.

Energy of Body

Reflection

Your body carries its own rhythm with peaks of vitality,
moments of steadiness, natural dips that ask for care.
Summer invites you to notice this rhythm
rather than fight it.
Energy flows best when it is respected.
Today is not about doing more,
but about noticing when your body feels most alive
and when it asks for support.

Affirmation

I listen to my body's natural rhythm.
I work with my energy, not against it.

Reflection Question

When does my body feel most energized today?

Energy of Emotion

Reflection

Emotions influence energy more than effort ever could.
Joy expands vitality. Resentment drains it.
Today invites you to notice
which emotions feel energizing
and which feel depleting without judgment.
Awareness gives you choice.
When emotions are acknowledged,
energy begins to move more freely.

Affirmation

I honor the emotions that fuel my vitality.

Reflection Question

Which emotion gives me energy right now?

Energy of Choice

Reflection

Energy is not meant to be spent all at once.
Summer growth thrives on sustainability.
Today invites you to choose effort that
you can maintain rather than effort that exhausts you.
Small, steady actions often carry more power
than bursts of intensity.

Affirmation

I choose effort that supports my vitality.

Reflection Question

What choice today supports sustainable energy?

Energy of Rest

Reflection

Rest is not the opposite of energy, it is its source. Summer reminds you that renewal happens when rest is welcomed rather than resisted. Today invites you to rest before exhaustion arrives. Proactive rest keeps vitality alive.

Affirmation

I allow rest to renew my energy.

Reflection Question

What kind of rest would support me most today?

Energy of Relationship

Reflection

Some connections energize you.
Others quietly drain you.
Today invites you to notice how your energy
responds in relationship,
Not to judge, but to understand.
Healthy connection supports vitality
through mutual presence and respect.

Affirmation

I honor connections that support my energy.

Reflection Question

Which connection feels most energizing right now?

Energy of Perception

Reflection

Perception shapes how energy is experienced.
When you notice subtle shifts
like fatigue, excitement, ease,
you can respond with care.
Today invites you to observe your energy levels
without labeling them good or bad.
Information leads to balance.

Affirmation

I notice and respond to my energy with awareness.

Reflection Question

What subtle energy shift can I notice today?

Energy of Trust

Reflection

Trust in Summer means believing that
your energy can be restored.
You do not need to hoard it or push it.
Today invites you to trust your body's ability
to replenish when given support.
Vitality is resilient.

Affirmation

I trust my capacity to renew and restore.
My energy supports my life.

Reflection Question

What would change if I trusted my energy more?

Energy
Circulating vitality without burning out

Embodiment Focus

Rhythmic activation
Nervous System Tone: Mobilization + safety

Practice

- Stand or sit upright

- Begin gently tapping your hands on your thighs or Chest in a slow, steady rhythm

- Inhale through the nose

- Exhale through the mouth while continuing the tapping

- Continue for 30–60 seconds, keeping the rhythm comfortable

Pause and notice the feeling of energy moving rather than building pressure.

Why This Supports Energy

Energy thrives on circulation, not force.
Rhythmic movement helps mobilize vitality while keeping the nervous system regulated, preventing the buildup that leads to exhaustion.

Let energy move through you, not consume you.

Truth made visible.

Expression

"Allowing what is within you to be seen."

In Summer, growth becomes visible. Expression is the natural outcome of what has been tended quietly. It does not require performance or perfection, only honesty.

You may feel called to speak, create, share, or move in new ways. Expression is not about approval; it is about alignment. Let what is alive within you find form without over-editing.

What you express does not need to be loud to be true.

Expression is growth made visible.

Expression of Body

Reflection

Your body expresses before words do.
Through posture, movement, and breath,
it reveals what is alive within you.
Today invites you to notice how your body
wants to move, stretch, or settle.
Expression through the body
does not require choreography, Only permission.

Affirmation

I allow my body to express itself naturally.

Reflection Question

How does my body want to express itself today?

Expression of Emotion

Reflection

Expression begins when emotions are allowed
to exist openly.
You do not need to amplify or minimize what you feel.
Today invites you to acknowledge
your emotions honestly, First to yourself.
Expression rooted in honesty creates relief and clarity.

Affirmation

I allow my emotions to be known without judgment.

Reflection Question

What feeling wants to be expressed right now?

Expression of Choice

Reflection

Expression is a choice.
You decide when and how to share what is alive within you.
Today invites you to choose expression that feels aligned,
not forced or withheld.
You are allowed to speak, create,
or remain quiet with intention.

Affirmation

I choose expression that feels true to me.

Reflection Question

What feels ready to be shared today?

Expression of Rest

Reflection

Holding back expression can be exhausting.
Today invites you to rest from over-editing yourself.
You do not need to perfect your expression before allowing it to exist.
Rest comes when authenticity replaces control.

Affirmation

I rest from overthinking my expression.

Reflection Question

Where can I stop editing myself today?

Expression of Relationship

Reflection

Expression deepens connection
when it is honest and respectful.
Today invites you to notice how your truth wants to be shared
in relationship without blame or expectation.
Expression is an offering, not a demand.

Affirmation

I express myself with honesty and care.

Reflection Question

What truth wants to be spoken gently today?

Expression of Perception

Reflection

Expression clarifies perception.
When you allow yourself to be seen,
you also see yourself more clearly.
Today invites you to notice how expressing truth
shifts your understanding of who you are.

Affirmation

I see myself clearly when I express honestly.

Reflection Question

How does expression change the way I see myself?

Expression of Trust

Reflection

Trusting expression means trusting that your voice
weather spoken or unspoken has value.
You do not need to justify your truth.
Today invites you to trust that what you express
belongs in the world.

Affirmation

I trust my voice and my expression.
What I share matters.

Reflection Question

What would it feel like to trust my voice fully?

Expression

Allowing Sound and Movement To Be Seen

Embodiment Focus

Safe expression
Nervous System Tone: Openness + confidence

Practice

- Stand or sit comfortably

- Take a slow inhale through the nose

- On the exhale, release a gentle sound, a hum, sigh, or soft vowel

- Let the sound be natural, not loud or shaped

- Repeat 3–5 times, noticing vibration in the chest or throat

After the final sound, sit quietly
and notice any sense of relief or openness.

Why This Supports Expression

Expression begins with the body's willingness to be heard. Sound-based release activates the vagus nerve and teaches the nervous system that expression can be safe, simple, and unforced.

Your voice does not need permission to exist.

Life touching life.

Connection

"Meeting others from fullness."

As life expands, connection becomes more available. Summer invites interaction, collaboration, and shared experience.

This theme is about how you meet others not from need, but from presence.

Connection deepens when you remain anchored in yourself. You are not required to give more than you have or shrink to be understood. Mutuality thrives when boundaries and openness coexist.

Let connection be nourishing, not consuming.

True connection honors both space and closeness.

Connection in Body

Reflection

Connection is felt in the body first.
A relaxed jaw, an open chest, a steady breath
when you feel safe with someone.
Today invites you to notice how your body
responds in connection.
Where it softens and where it tightens.
These signals offer guidance without judgment.

Affirmation

I listen to my body's signals in connection.

Reflection Question

How does my body feel when I'm truly
at ease with someone?

Connection of Emotion

Reflection

Connection deepens when emotions are available
rather than guarded.
This does not mean sharing everything,
it means allowing yourself to feel honestly
in the presence of others.
Today invites you to notice where
emotional openness feels supportive
and where it feels premature.

Affirmation

I allow emotional openness at my own pace.

Reflection Question

Where does emotional availability feel safe today?

Connection of Choice

Reflection

Healthy connection is mutual.
Today invites you to choose relationships
where giving and receiving are balanced.
You are not required to carry connection alone.
Mutuality creates sustainability and ease.

Affirmation

I choose connections rooted in mutual respect.

Reflection Question

Where can I choose mutuality today?

Connection of Rest

Reflection

Connection does not always require
conversation or activity.
Sometimes presence itself is enough.
Today invites you to rest in togetherness,
allowing silence or simplicity
to support connection without effort.

Affirmation

I allow connection to be simple and restful.

Reflection Question

Where can I enjoy shared presence
without doing more?

Connection of Relationship

Reflection

Boundaries make connection safe.
Today invites you to honor your limits
without apology and to respect the limits of others.
Clear boundaries allow connection
to deepen without overwhelm.

Affirmation

I honor boundaries as a foundation for connection.

Reflection Question

What boundary supports connection right now?

Connection of Perception

Reflection

Connection deepens when perception is clear.
Today invites you to see others as they are,
not as you hope or fear them to be.
Clear seeing reduces misunderstanding
and creates honesty.

Affirmation

I see others clearly and compassionately.

Reflection Question

What changes when I release
assumptions about someone?

Connection of Trust

Reflection

Trust in connection grows when you allow
shared space to be what it is:
dynamic, imperfect, and alive.
Today invites you to trust that connection
can evolve without constant management.

Affirmation

I trust connection to unfold naturally.
I allow space for growth together.

Reflection Question

Where can I trust connection without controlling it?

Connection

Being With Others Without Losing Yourself

Embodiment Focus

Relational presence
Nervous System Tone: Safety + openness

Practice

Stand or sit facing forward

Place one hand on your heart, one hand on your lower belly

Take a slow inhale

As you exhale, gently extend one arm forward, palm open

Return the arm and repeat 3 times, alternating sides

Pause and notice the feeling of reaching outward while staying connected inward.

Why This Supports Connection

Healthy connection requires both openness and self-contact. This practice teaches the body how to extend toward others without abandoning its own center.

Connection begins when you stay with yourself.

Lightness without reason.

Joy

"Letting pleasure count."

Joy is often treated as optional or secondary. Summer reminds you that joy is vital. It restores energy, softens effort, and reminds you why growth matters.

Joy does not need to be earned. It can be simple, fleeting, or quiet. Allow yourself to notice what feels good without minimizing it.

Pleasure is not a distraction from growth, It is part of it.

Joy nourishes what effort alone cannot

Joy of Body

Reflection

Joy often lives in the body before it becomes a thought.
A spontaneous smile.
A relaxed breath.
A feeling of ease moving through you.
Today invites you to notice where your body experiences delightwithout minimizing it.
Joy does not need to be practical to be meaningful.

Affirmation

I allow my body to experience joy freely.

Reflection Question

Where does my body feel a sense of ease or delight today?

Joy of Emotion

Reflection

Joy softens the emotional landscape.
It does not erase difficulty, it balances it.
Today invites you to notice moments
of lightness, even if they are brief.
Joy does not need to be constant to be real.

Affirmation

I allow moments of joy to exist
alongside everything else.

Reflection Question

What moment brought me a sense of lightness today?

Joy of Choice

Reflection

Joy can be chosen: not forced, but allowed.
Today invites you to choose enjoyment
where it is available.
You are not required to postpone joy
until everything is resolved.
Pleasure is part of being alive.

Affirmation

I choose to allow enjoyment into my day.

Reflection Question

Where can I choose enjoyment today?

Joy of Rest

Reflection

Joy deepens when you allow yourself to linger.
Today invites you to rest into moments
that feel good rather than rushing past them.
Let pleasure settle into your nervous system
as nourishment.

Affirmation

I allow myself to rest within joyful moments.

Reflection Question

What feels good enough to linger with today?

Joy of Relationship

Reflection

Joy expands when it is shared.
Laughter, warmth, and simple enjoyment
strengthen connection.
Today invites you to notice where joy naturally arises
in relationship without trying to manufacture it.

Affirmation

I allow joy to flow through my connections.

Reflection Question

Who or what brings out joy in me naturally?

Joy of Perception

Reflection

Joy sharpens perception.
You may notice beauty in small, ordinary moments.
Today invites you to look for what is pleasant, colorful,
or comforting without dismissing it as insignificant.

Affirmation

I notice beauty in the everyday.

Reflection Question

What small beauty can I appreciate today?

Joy of Trust

Reflection

Some people hesitate to trust joy,
fearing it may disappear.
Today invites you to trust joy
as a natural part of life's rhythm.
You do not need to hold onto it tightly.
Joy knows how to return.

Affirmation

I trust joy to come and go naturally.
I allow myself to receive it.

Reflection Question

What would change if I trusted joy more fully?

Joy

Letting Pleasure Move Through the Body

Embodiment Focus

Spontaneous enjoyment
Nervous System Tone: Safety + lightness

Practice

- Stand comfortably and gently bounce your knees, just enough to create a soft rhythm

- Let your arms swing loosely at your sides

- Allow a small smile to form, without forcing it

- Take 3–5 natural breaths, staying with the light movement

After stopping, notice any warmth, ease, or subtle uplift in your body.

Why This Supports Joy

Joy is a bodily response before it is an emotion. Light, rhythmic movement signals safety and aliveness to the nervous system, allowing joy to arise naturally rather than being pursued or manufactured.

Joy arrives when the body feels free to move.

Protection that allows growth.

Essential Boundaries

"Protecting what sustains you"

Knowing what must be protected for growth to continue.
Summer offers abundance, energy, connection, opportunity, expression.
But abundance without discernment leads to depletion.
Essential boundaries are not restrictions placed out of fear;
they are protections chosen from wisdom.

These boundaries arise naturally when you are present with your energy. You begin to sense what is essential to preserve—your time, your body, your emotional capacity, your inner clarity. Essential boundaries are not rigid lines; they are living agreements with yourself that evolve as you do.

In this season, boundaries are not about saying no to life. They are about saying yes to what sustains you. When boundaries are essential, they feel grounding rather than defensive. They allow joy to continue without collapse, connection without exhaustion, and growth without loss of self.

Essential boundaries do not require explanation. They are felt internally as relief, steadiness, and self-respect.

What you protect with intention is what continues to grow.

Essential Boundaries Of Body

Reflection

Your body communicates boundaries
clearly through fatigue, tension, or ease.
Today invites you to listen without judgment.
Limits are not obstacles; they are information.
When you honor your body's signals,
energy becomes steadier and more available.

Affirmation

I respect my body's limits with care.

Reflection Question

What signal is my body offering me today?

Essential Boundaries Of Emotion

Reflection

Emotional boundaries protect your inner world.
You are not meant to process everything
at once or carry emotions that are not yours.
Today invites you to notice what feels
emotionally manageable and what feels overwhelming.
Honoring capacity is an act of self-respect.

Affirmation

I honor my emotional capacity.

Reflection Question

What emotion feels like it needs space right now?

Essential Boundaries of Rest

Reflection

Constant availability is exhausting.
Today invites you to rest from being reachable
or responsive at all times.
Boundaries around rest preserve energy and clarity.
Stepping back briefly allows you to return with
presence.

Affirmation

I allow myself to be unavailable when I need rest.

Reflection Question

Where can I step back without guilt?

Essential Boundaries of Choice

Reflection

Every yes shapes your energy.
Boundaries help you choose wisely.
Today invites you to consider
where a clear yes supports your vitality
and where a gentle no creates relief.
You are allowed to choose alignment over obligation.

Affirmation

I choose yes and no with intention.

Reflection Question

Where does a boundary create more ease today?

Essential Boundaries of Relationship

Reflection

Healthy relationships respect limits.
Today invites you to notice how boundaries
support trust and safety rather than distance.
Clear boundaries create space for genuine connection.

Affirmation

I express my boundaries with clarity and care.

Reflection Question

What boundary strengthens a relationship right now?

Essential Boundaries of Perception

Reflection

Boundaries are often misunderstood as restriction.
Today invites you to see them as support structures
that are holding growth steady.
When perception shifts,
boundaries feel empowering rather than limiting.

Affirmation

I see boundaries as support, not limitation.

Reflection Question

How does my perspective change
when I view boundaries as care?

Essential Boundaries of Trust

Reflection

Trusting boundaries means believing
you can honor them without justification.
Today invites you to trust your ability to protect
what matter even when it feels uncomfortable.
Growth thrives within held edges.

Affirmation

I trust myself to honor my boundaries.
I protect my energy with confidence.

Reflection Question

What boundary am I ready to trust myself with?

Essential Boundaries

Creating a container for energy

Embodiment Focus

Containment without restriction
Nervous System Tone: Safety + clarity

Practice

- Stand with your feet hip-width apart

- Slowly trace an invisible circle around your body with your hands, as if outlining your personal space

- Keep the movement slow and intentional

- Once complete, rest your hands lightly on your hips or lower belly

- Take 3 steady breaths, feeling the space you occupy

Pause and notice the sensation of having edges without tension.

Why This Supports Essential Boundaries

Boundaries are not walls, they are containers. This practice helps the body sense its own perimeter, reinforcing that energy can stay regulated when it knows where it belongs.

Boundaries allow energy to remain sustainable.

Standing fully where you are.

Confidence in Presence

"Trusting yourself without performance"

Standing comfortably in who you are, right here Confidence in Summer does not ask you to be louder, bolder, or more impressive. It asks you to be here. Fully. Honestly. Without apology.

This kind of confidence grows from presence rather than comparison. It forms when you stop reaching for approval and begin inhabiting yourself as you are. Breath steadies. The body relaxes. There is less effort spent managing perception and more ease in simply being.

Confidence in presence does not need to announce itself. It is felt in grounded stillness, in clear boundaries, in the absence of urgency to prove. You may notice that you listen more than you speak, move with less hesitation, and respond rather than react. In Summer, presence becomes strength. When you are fully here, you do not need to be anything else. Confidence arises naturally when you trust the space you occupy.

You do not need to perform to belong.

Presence is enough.

Confidence In Presence of Body

Reflection

Confidence in the body feels like
ease rather than tension.
Shoulders drop. Breath steadies.
Movement feels natural instead of guarded.
Today invites you to notice how your body
carries itself when it feels safe to be seen.
Confidence does not require stiffness,
it thrives in comfort.

Affirmation

I allow my body to relax into confidence.

Reflection Question

Where does my body feel more at ease than before?

Confidence In Presence of Emotion

Reflection

Emotional confidence grows when you trust yourself
to feel what you feel without overreaction.
Today invites you to notice emotional steadiness
and less need to defend, explain, or prove.
Confidence does not erase emotion;
it holds it with assurance.

Affirmation

I trust myself to navigate my emotions.

Reflection Question

What emotion feels easier to hold now?

Confidence In Presence of Choice

Reflection

Confidence is reinforced through choice.
When you make decisions aligned with your values,
self-trust deepens.
Today invites you to choose from inner authority
rather than external validation.
You are allowed to trust your judgment.

Affirmation

I choose from inner authority and clarity.

Reflection Question

Where can I choose based on self-trust today?

Confidence In Presence of Rest

Reflection

Confidence strengthens when you
stop striving to be different.
Today invites you to rest in who you are
without comparison or self-improvement.
Resting in identity allows confidence
to feel stable rather than conditional.

Affirmation

I rest in who I am without needing to change.

Reflection Question

Where can I stop trying and simply be today?

Confidence In Presence of Relationship

Reflection

Confident connection does not require overgiving. Today invites you to notice how presence alone can be enough. You do not need to earn belonging through effort. Authenticity strengthens trust.

Affirmation

I show up as myself without overgiving.

Reflection Question

Where can I allow presence to be enough?

Confidence In Presence of Perception

Reflection

Confidence grows when perception aligns with reality.
Today invites you to see yourself as
you are capable, learning, and whole.
You do not need to inflate
or diminish yourself to belong.

Affirmation

I see myself with honesty and respect.

Reflection Question

What truth about myself can I acknowledge today?

Confidence In Presence of Trust

Reflection

At its core, confidence is trust.
Trust that your presence matters.
Today invites you to trust your light
without needing permission.
You do not take away from others
by standing fully as yourself.

Affirmation

I trust my light and allow it to be seen.
I stand confidently in who I am.

Reflection Question

What would it feel like to trust my light completely?

Confidence In Presence

Remaining grounded while being seen

Embodiment Focus

Steady visibility
Nervous System Tone: Safety + self-trust

Practice

- Stand upright with feet firmly planted

- Place one hand on your heart, one hand at your side

- Lift your chin slightly, allowing the chest to remain open

- Take 3 slow breaths, keeping your gaze forward and relaxed

After the final breath,
notice the feeling of being visible without bracing.

Why This Supports Confidence in Presence

Confidence in Summer is not about assertion — it is about remaining connected to yourself while engaging the world. This posture-based practice teaches the nervous system that being seen can feel steady and safe.

You can be present without performing.

Movement without outcome.

Play

"Inviting lightness into growth."

Play brings balance to intensity. It reminds you that not everything needs to be serious to be meaningful.

In Summer, play reintroduces curiosity and movement without outcome.

You may feel drawn to spontaneity, creativity, or rest that feels joyful. Play loosens rigidity and restores flow.
Growth thrives when there is room to enjoy the process.

Play keeps life responsive and alive

Play of Body

Reflection

Play often begins in the body as movement without purpose,
Stretching, dancing, walking without destination.
Today invites you to let your body move simply
because it wants to.
There is no goal to reach and nothing to optimize.
Movement becomes play when it is free.

Affirmation

I allow my body to move with freedom and ease.

Reflection Question

How does my body want to move today
without purpose?

Play of Emotion

Reflection

Play brings emotional relief.
It softens seriousness and invites joy
without explanation.
Today asks you to notice where lightness wants to enter.
Maybe it's through laughter, curiosity, or ease.
You are not betraying depth by enjoying yourself.
Play restores it.

Affirmation

I allow lightness to coexist with depth.

Reflection Question

What helps me feel emotionally lighter today?

Play of Choice

Reflection

Play is a choice to explore without outcome. Today invites you to choose curiosity instead of productivity, interest instead of result. When you release the need to gain something, experience itself becomes rewarding.

Affirmation

I choose curiosity without expectation.

Reflection Question

Where can I explore without needing a result?

Play of Rest

Reflection

Playful rest feels different from collapse.
It is restorative because it engages delight
rather than withdrawal.
Today invites you to rest in ways
that feel enjoyable with music, nature, creativity,
or simple pleasure.

Affirmation

I allow rest to feel enjoyable and nourishing.

Reflection Question

What kind of rest feels playful today?

Play of Relationships

Reflection

Play deepens connection through shared
joy and spontaneity.
Today invites you to let connection be light:
less serious, less managed.
Laughter and presence often create closeness
more easily than effort.

Affirmation

I allow playfulness to strengthen my connections.

Reflection Question

Who do I feel most playful and at ease with?

Play of Perception

Reflection

Play shifts perception.
Life becomes an invitation rather than a task.
Today invites you to notice moments that could
be approached with curiosity instead of control.
When perception loosens, experience expands.

Affirmation

I see life as an invitation to engage.

Reflection Question

What moment could I approach with more playfulness?

Play of Trust

Reflection

Play requires trust.
The trust that enjoyment does not derail growth.
Today invites you to trust that
joy and lightness are not distractions,
but vital elements of a well-lived life.
Growth thrives when it is enjoyed.

Affirmation

I trust play to support my growth.
Joy is safe to welcome.

Reflection Question

What would change if I trusted joy more fully?

Play

Inviting spontaneity

Embodiment Focus

Improvised movement
Nervous System Tone: Freedom + regulation

Practice

Stand or sit and allow your body to move in any way it wishes for 30–60 seconds

There is no right movement — stretching, swaying, rolling shoulders, or small gestures are all welcome

Keep the breath natural and the movement light

When finished, pause and notice any sense of ease or openness.

Why This Supports Play

Play restores flexibility to both body and mind. Unstructured movement reminds the nervous system that freedom does not require chaos — it can exist within safety and awareness.

Play reconnects you to possibility.

What grows to be shared.

Contribution

"Sharing from abundance."

When growth matures, it naturally wants to give. Contribution in Summer is not obligation, it is overflow. It arises when you feel resourced enough to share.

This may look like offering support, insight, presence, or creativity. Contribution feels best when it is chosen freely and given without depletion.

What you offer matters when it comes from fullness.

Giving is sustainable when it is rooted in enough

Contribution of Body

Reflection

When the body feels resourced, giving feels natural.
Energy moves outward without strain:
through help, touch, effort, or presence.
Today invites you to notice when giving
feels light rather than depleting.
Contribution rooted in the body's wisdom
is generous and sustainable.

Affirmation

I give from a place of vitality and ease.

Reflection Question

Where does giving feel natural and unforced today?

Contribution of Emotion

Reflection

Contribution includes emotional presence
like listening, empathy, and care.
When emotions are not overextended,
generosity feels steady rather than draining.
Today invites you to notice
what you can offer emotionally without self-sacrifice.

Affirmation

I offer emotional generosity without depletion.

Reflection Question

What emotional support feels available to offer today?

Contribution of Choice

Reflection

You choose how and where you contribute.
Today invites you to make conscious choices
about your giving, Aligning contribution
with capacity and intention.
Giving is most powerful when it is chosen freely.

Affirmation

I choose contribution that aligns with my capacity.

Reflection Question

What kind of contribution feels aligned right now?

Contribution of Rest

Reflection

Even meaningful contribution requires rest.
Today invites you to pause before depletion appears.
Rest protects the quality of what you give.
Sustainable contribution honors recovery.

Affirmation

I rest to preserve the quality of my giving.

Reflection Question

Where do I need rest to continue giving well?

Contribution of Relationship

Reflection

Healthy contribution in relationship is mutual.
Today invites you to notice
where giving and receiving feel balanced.
You are not meant to pour endlessly.
Connection thrives when contribution flows both ways.

Affirmation

I allow contribution to be mutual and balanced.

Reflection Question

Where does reciprocity feel present in my connections?

Contribution of Perception

Reflection

You may not always see the effects of what you offer.
Today invites you to trust
that your presence, kindness, and effort matter.
Even when outcomes are subtle.
Contribution often works quietly.

Affirmation

I recognize the value of my presence.

Reflection Question

What impact might my presence
have that I haven't noticed?

Contribution of Trust

Reflection

True contribution flows from overflow, not obligation.
Today invites you to trust that when you are nourished,
giving happens naturally.
You do not need to force generosity,
it arises when you are whole.

Affirmation

I trust abundance to flow through me.
I give from overflow.

Reflection Question

What would change if I trusted my capacity to give naturally?

Contribution

Offering without depletion

Embodiment Focus

Giving from fullness
Nervous System Tone: Safety + generosity

Practice

- Stand or sit comfortably

- Place one hand on your heart

- On the inhale, draw the elbow of that arm slightly inward toward your body

- On the exhale, gently extend the arm forward, palm open

- Move slowly and repeat 3–5 times, alternating arms if desired

After the final movement, pause and notice the difference between offering from fullness versus effort.

Why This Supports Contribution

Healthy contribution begins with self-connection. This practice teaches the body to give outward while remaining rooted inward, preventing overextension and reinforcing sustainability.

You give best when you remain connected to yourself.

Choosing what continues.

Discernment

"Noticing when to pause."

Even in abundance, wisdom knows when to slow down. Discernment is the ability to sense what is no longer aligned even if it once was.

Summer discernment helps you adjust course before burnout sets in. It asks you to listen to subtle signals and respond with care.

Expansion is healthiest when it includes moments of pause.

Listening is a form of leadership.

Discernment of Body

Reflection

Your body often senses
what the mind tries to override.
Subtle fatigue, tightness, or restlessness can signal
that something needs adjustment.
Today invites you to listen
without pushing past these cues.
Discernment in the body is not limitation,
it is intelligent self-regulation.

Affirmation

I listen to my body's signals with respect.

Reflection Question

What is my body quietly communicating right now?

Discernment of Emotion

Reflection

Discernment brings emotional clarity.
You may notice when enthusiasm shifts to obligation,
or when care turns into resentment.
Today invites you to honor
emotional information without judgment.
Feelings help guide wise decisions
when they are acknowledged.

Affirmation

I honor emotional signals as guidance.

Reflection Question

What emotion is offering me information today?

Discernment of Choice

Reflection

Not every opportunity requires a yes.
Discernment allows you to choose
based on alignment rather than momentum.
Today invites you to pause before deciding
and to notice what choice
feels most supportive of your well-being.

Affirmation

I choose with wisdom and clarity.

Reflection Question

What decision could benefit from a pause today?

Discernment of Rest

Reflection

Discernment recognizes the value of rest
before exhaustion arrives.
Today invites you to rest proactively
rather than reactively.
Pausing early preserves energy
and clarity for what truly matters.

Affirmation

I allow rest to prevent depletion.

Reflection Question

Where can I rest before I feel drained?

Discernment of Relationship

Reflection

Wise connection honors both closeness and space. Today invites you to notice where interaction feels nourishing and where it feels heavy. Discernment in relationship allows you to stay open without overextending.

Affirmation

I honor discernment in my relationships.

Reflection Question

Which connection feels most aligned right now?

Discernment of Perception

Reflection

Discernment sharpens perception.
You begin to see what supports your growth
and what distracts from it.
Today invites you to observe without urgency.
Clear seeing creates ease.

Affirmation

I see clearly what serves me now.

Reflection Question

What feels less aligned than it once did?

Discernment of Trust

Reflection

At its heart, discernment is trust.
Trust in your inner wisdom to guide you
without constant analysis.
Today invites you to trust your ability
to sense what is enough,
what is complete,
and what deserves your energy.

Affirmation

I trust my inner wisdom to guide me.
I pause when clarity asks.

Reflection Question

What inner knowing am I ready to trust?

Discernment

Listening for what is true

Embodiment Focus

Sensory clarity
Nervous System Tone: Regulation + choice

Practice

- Sit or stand comfortably

- Slowly turn your head slightly to one side

- Pause and notice any bodily response : ease, tension, neutrality

- Return to center, then repeat on the other side

- Move through 3–5 gentle rounds, staying curious rather than evaluative

Afterward, notice how the body communicates clarity without words.

Why This Supports Discernment

Discernment is a felt sense before it becomes a decision. This practice strengthens the body's ability to notice subtle signals, supporting choices that feel aligned rather than forced.

Your body knows before your mind decides.

Poise in motion.

Balance

"Regulating energy with intention."

Balance is dynamic, not fixed. In Summer, balance means adjusting as conditions change. Some days ask for action. Others ask for rest.

Rather than striving for consistency, allow yourself to respond to what is needed now. Balance supports longevity.

You are allowed to recalibrate.

Balance is responsiveness, not rigidity.

Balance of Body

Reflection

Balance in the body is rhythmic, not rigid. It adjusts moment by moment then activity followed by rest, engagement followed by release. Today invites you to notice your natural rhythm and support it rather than forcing consistency. Balance emerges when you listen.

Affirmation

I honor my body's natural rhythm.

Reflection Question

What rhythm does my body need today?

Balance of Emotion

Reflection

Emotional balance does not mean neutrality.
It means allowing feelings to move
without tipping into overwhelm or suppression.
Today invites you to notice where emotions
can be felt and released with care.
Balance creates steadiness without dulling experience.

Affirmation

I allow my emotions to move in healthy rhythm.

Reflection Question

What emotion needs gentle regulation right now?

Balance of Choice

Reflection

Balance requires on going adjustment.
Today invites you to choose
responsiveness over perfection.
Small shifts, less here, more there restore alignment.
Balance is not achieved once; it is practiced.

Affirmation

I choose flexibility to maintain balance.

Reflection Question

What small adjustment could bring more ease today?

Balance of Rest

Reflection

Rest recalibrates balance.
It restores clarity and steadies energy.
Today invites you to rest not as escape,
but as tuning bringing yourself back into alignment
with what you need now.

Affirmation

I use rest to recalibrate my energy.

Reflection Question

What kind of rest would restore balance today?

Balance of Relationship

Reflection

Balance in relationship honors
both togetherness and autonomy.
Today invites you to notice where connection
feels nourishing and where space supports clarity.
Balance allows relationships to breathe.

Affirmation

I honor balance in my relationships.

Reflection Question

Where does space or closeness feel most supportive?

Balance of Perception

Reflection

Balance shifts perception away from extremes.
Today invites you to notice the middle ground
where effort and ease coexist.
Seeing nuance reduces pressure
and supports wise response.

Affirmation

I see balance as dynamic and supportive.

Reflection Question

Where can I soften an all-or-nothing view?

Balance of Trust

Reflection

Balance ultimately rests on trust.
Trust that rhythm will guide you if you listen.
Today invites you to trust your ability to regulate,
adjust, and return to center as needed.

Affirmation

I trust my natural rhythm to guide me.
Balance returns when I listen.

Reflection Question

What would it feel like to trust my rhythm fully?

Balance

Finding center while shifting

Embodiment Focus

Dynamic stability
Nervous System Tone: Safety + adaptability

Practice

- Stand with feet hip-width apart

- Slowly lift one foot just an inch off the ground

- Hold for one breath, then gently lower

- Switch sides

- Repeat 2–3 times per side, moving slowly

Afterward, stand with both feet grounded and notice the sense of equilibrium.

Why This Supports Balance

Balance is not stillness, it is the ability to recover. This practice teaches the nervous system how to remain regulated through small shifts, reinforcing confidence in adjustment.

Balance is the art of returning to center.

Recognizing what has been given.

Gratitude

"Recognizing abundance without clinging."

Gratitude in Summer is spacious.

It notices what is present without fearing its loss. This theme invites you to acknowledge what is working, what is supportive, and what has grown.

Gratitude does not require perfection. It simply asks for recognition.

What you appreciate becomes more integrated.

Gratitude grounds abundance.

Gratitude of Body

Reflection

Gratitude lives in the body as ease.
A relaxed jaw.
A softened belly.
A breath that drops lower.
Today invites you to notice where your body
feels supported, nourished, or relieved.
Gratitude does not require comparison,
only presence with what is sustaining you now.

Affirmation

I allow my body to receive what supports it.

Reflection Question

Where does my body feel supported or at ease today?

Gratitude of Emotion

Reflection

Gratitude does not deny difficulty, it coexists with it. Today invites you to notice an emotion that feels steady, comforting, or quietly positive. Appreciation deepens when you allow yourself to acknowledge what feels good without fearing its loss.

Affirmation

I allow appreciation to exist alongside all emotions.

Reflection Question

What emotion feels quietly supportive right now?

Gratitude of Choice

Reflection

Gratitude can be chosen as a lens.
Today invites you to choose appreciation
where it feels authentic, not forced.
You are not required to be grateful for everything.
Choosing what to appreciate
keeps gratitude honest and grounding.

Affirmation

I choose appreciation with honesty and ease.

Reflection Question

What feels genuinely worthy of appreciation today?

Gratitude of Rest

Reflection

Gratitude deepens when you rest in the sense of enough.
Today invites you to pause striving
and allow what is present to be sufficient.
Resting in enough does not limit growth, it stabilizes it.

Affirmation

I rest in the feeling of enough.

Reflection Question

Where can I pause and feel contentment today?

Gratitude of Relationship

Reflection

Appreciation strengthens relationships when it is felt rather than performed. Today invites you to notice someone whose presence supports you without needing to say or do anything extra. Gratitude can be quiet and still be real.

Affirmation

I appreciate the connections that nourish me.

Reflection Question

Who or what feels supportive in my life right now?

Gratitude of Perception

Reflection

Gratitude refines perception.
You may begin to notice abundance
in simple, ordinary moments.
Today invites you to see
what is working, flowing, or available
without needing it to be extraordinary.

Affirmation

I see abundance in the present moment.

Reflection Question

What is quietly abundant in my life today?

Gratitude of Trust

Reflection

Gratitude becomes complete when it is trusted
when you believe that what supports you
now is not accidental.
Today invites you to trust the sufficiency
of this moment without clinging to it.
What is meant to continue will.

Affirmation

I trust what is here to support me.
I allow gratitude to soften my grip.

Reflection Question

What would change if I trusted
this moment to be enough?

Gratitude

Receiving what is already here

Embodiment Focus

Opening to receive
Nervous System Tone: Safety + contentment

Practice

- Sit or stand comfortably

- Place both hands over your heart

- Take a slow inhale through the nose

- As you exhale, soften the shoulders and chest

- With each breath, silently notice one sensation of comfort or ease

- Repeat 3–5 breaths, keeping attention gentle

After the final breath, rest in stillness for a moment.

Why This Supports Gratitude

Gratitude is not a thought practice, it is a receiving state. This embodiment invites the nervous system to register safety and sufficiency, allowing appreciation to arise naturally.

Gratitude grows when the body feels enough

Ready, not rushed.

Maturity

"Preparing to refine and release."

As Summer draws toward Autumn, maturity emerges. This is the understanding that not everything needs to continue unchanged. Growth evolves.

Maturity invites you to carry forward what is sustainable and prepare to let go of what has served its purpose.
There is no urgency, only readiness.

You are not losing anything. You are refining.

Expansion becomes wisdom when guided by maturity.

Maturity of Body

Reflection

Maturity shows up in the body as knowing
when to slow, when to stop, and when to transition.
You may notice a desire for steadier movement,
deeper rest, or quieter rhythms.
Today invites you to listen
to what your body is signaling not as decline,
but as wisdom guiding the next phase.

Affirmation

I honor my body's signals as wisdom.

Reflection Question

What shift is my body asking for right now?

Maturity of Emotion

Reflection

Maturity brings emotional honesty.
It allows you to acknowledge satisfaction alongside fatigue,
gratitude alongside readiness to let go.
Today invites you to hold complexity
without forcing resolution.
Emotional maturity makes room
for mixed feelings without judgment.

Affirmation

I allow emotional truth to be complex and whole.

Reflection Question

What mixed emotions can I acknowledge today?

Maturity of Choice

Reflection

Not everything that grew in Summer
needs to carry forward unchanged.
Maturity invites discernment
about what continues and what completes.
Today invites you to choose what still feels aligned
without guilt for what is ready to be released.

Affirmation

I choose continuation and completion with clarity.

Reflection Question

What feels ready to continue and what feels complete?

Maturity of Rest

Reflection

Transitions are supported by rest.
Today invites you to pause
before moving into the next season.
Rest here is not withdrawal, it is integration.
Let what you've lived this season settle gently.

Affirmation

I allow rest to support transition.

Reflection Question

Where can I pause before moving forward?

Maturity of Relationship

Reflection

Maturity in relationship honors
truth, space, and respect.
Today invites you to notice where relationships
feel steady and where they ask for recalibration.
Mature connection allows change without drama.

Affirmation

I honor maturity in my relationships.

Reflection Question

Which relationship feels ready for refinement?

Maturity of Perception

Reflection

Maturity refines perception.
You can see the season for what it was:
its gifts, its limits, its lessons without idealizing
or diminishing it.
Today invites you to look back
with clear, compassionate eyes.

Affirmation

I see this season clearly and honestly.

Reflection Question

What truth about this season can I acknowledge?

Maturity of Trust

Reflection

The final act of Summer maturity is trust.
Trust that releasing what has served
creates space for what comes next.
You are not losing momentum;
you are refining direction.
Today invites you to trust
the natural turning of the cycle.

Affirmation

I trust the wisdom of transition.
I release with gratitude and readiness.

Reflection Question

What am I ready to release as this season turns?

Maturity

Holding strength with softness

Embodiment Focus

Integrated presence
Nervous System Tone: Stability + wisdom

Practice

- Stand or sit upright with ease

- Lengthen the spine gently

- Place one hand on your heart, one hand on your thigh

- Take 3 slow, steady breaths, allowing both strength and softness to coexist

- Keep your gaze forward, relaxed and steady

After the final breath, notice the feeling of calm confidence without tension.

Why This Supports Maturity

Maturity is not hardness, it is integration. This practice allows strength and gentleness to exist together, teaching the nervous system that steadiness does not require rigidity.

Maturity lives where strength and softness meet.

Crossing the Threshold

From Summer into Autumn
Gathering What Has Grown

Summer invites fullness. It brings light, movement, connection, and the courage to be seen. Over this season, energy was expressed outward—through action, creativity, relationships, and presence. Some days felt expansive and alive. Others may have asked more than you expected. Both are part of abundance.

As Summer softens into Autumn, the focus shifts. This is the season of gathering—not everything, but what truly matters. Nature does not cling to every leaf. It selects, releases, and preserves with quiet intelligence. You are invited to do the same.

Before moving forward, pause to acknowledge what this season offered you. Notice what felt sustainable and what felt draining. Wisdom grows when you allow yourself to choose differently, informed by experience rather than expectation.

Autumn does not ask you to diminish your light. It asks you to refine it. What you carry forward now will shape the seasons ahead.

Crossing the Threshold

Guided Reflection Questions
Move through these slowly.
Let your answers be honest, not ideal.

What felt most alive for me during Summer?

Where did I feel stretched beyond what was sustainable?

What did I enjoy expressing or sharing?

What patterns became clear through experience?

What am I grateful for from this season?

What feels ready to be released with care?

Refining the Harvest

Use this page to reflect in whatever way feels natural.

One lesson Summer taught me:

One strength I discovered or strengthened:

One commitment I am ready to loosen or let go of:

Autumn

Integration & Release
The Season of Discernment

Autumn is the season of integration. It is a time to gather what has been learned, to release what is no longer needed, and to simplify with honesty and care. Autumn teaches us that letting go is not loss — it is wisdom in motion.

This season invites reflection without judgment. It asks you to look clearly at what has served you, what has changed, and what is ready to be laid down. Autumn honors completion, boundaries, and responsibility — not as heaviness, but as self-respect.

Here you will explore themes of awareness, evaluation, gratitude, release, simplification, wisdom, boundaries, responsibility, integrity, preservation, completion, and integration. T
hese themes support the process of harvesting insight while conserving energy for what comes next.

Autumn does not rush the ending.
It teaches you how to leave with grace.

Autumn Ritual

Honoring the Harvest

Autumn arrives with clarity. The air cools, the light softens, and the world begins to reveal what has truly endured. This is not a season of taking away—it is a season of choosing wisely. Nature gathers what is ready, releases what has completed its purpose, and trusts the rhythm of change.

This ritual invites you to do the same.

Begin by finding a quiet place where you can sit comfortably. Allow your body to settle. Let your shoulders soften and your breath slow naturally.

Take a deep breath in.
And a slow breath out.

Bring your attention to the past season. Notice what you invested energy in, what grew stronger, and what asked more of you than it gave back. There is no judgment here—only information. Wisdom forms when you allow experience to speak.

Now imagine yourself holding a basket. Gently place into it the moments, efforts, and qualities that feel nourishing and true. These are the things worth carrying forward. Next, acknowledge what no longer belongs in the basket. Thank it for what it taught you, and allow it to fall away without resistance.

Autumn does not cling. It trusts.

Take one final breath.
Feel the steadiness that remains when you choose with intention.

What you honor with gratitude
can be released with peace.
What remains is enough.

Noticing what is changing.

Awareness

Seeing clearly what is present

Autumn sharpens perception. As the light softens and the pace slows, details become easier to notice. Awareness in this season is about seeing what is actually here without exaggeration or avoidance.

You may notice patterns that were invisible before, or truths that feel ready to be acknowledged. Awareness is not judgment. It is simply attention. When you see clearly, you are better able to choose wisely.

Clarity begins with honest observation

Awareness of Body

Reflection

As the pace slows, the body becomes more honest.
Tension, ease, fatigue, and steadiness all speak clearly
when you allow yourself to listen.
Today invites you to notice what your body
is communicating without trying to fix it.
Awareness begins with recognition, not correction.

Affirmation

I listen to my body with clarity and respect.

Reflection Question

What is my body clearly communicating right now?

Awareness of Emotion

Reflection

Autumn awareness invites emotional honesty.
You may notice feelings you
once bypassed or softened.
This is not regression, it is clarity.
Today invites you to acknowledge what you feel
without labeling it good or bad.
When emotions are seen clearly,
they lose the need to demand attention.

Affirmation

I allow my emotions to be seen as they are.

Reflection Question

What emotion am I ready to acknowledge honestly?

Awareness of Choice

Reflection

Awareness is a choice.
You can turn toward what is present
or continue moving past it.
Today invites you to choose seeing over avoiding,
even if what you see feels uncomfortable.
Clarity creates freedom.

Affirmation

I choose clarity over avoidance.

Reflection Question

What am I choosing to see more clearly today?

Awareness of Rest

Reflection

Distraction dulls awareness.
Today invites you to rest
from unnecessary noise internal or external.
When you allow stillness, awareness sharpens naturally.
You do not need to search for insight.
It appears when space is created.

Affirmation

I rest from distraction and return to clarity.

Reflection Question

What distraction can I release today to see more clearly?

Awareness of Relationship

Reflection

Autumn awareness brings clarity to relationships.
You may notice patterns, dynamics, or truths
that were easier to overlook during busier seasons.
Today invites you to observe connection as it is,
not as you wish it to be.
Awareness supports wise response.

Affirmation

I see my relationships with honesty and compassion.

Reflection Question

What truth about a relationship is becoming clearer?

Awareness of Perception

Reflection

Awareness deepens when you release interpretation. Today invites you to notice what is happening without adding story, blame, or justification. Clear perception reduces emotional charge and restores steadiness.

Affirmation

I see what is present without distortion.

Reflection Question

What changes when I observe without adding meaning?

Awareness of Trust

Reflection

Trust in Autumn means trusting clarity
even when it asks for change.
Seeing clearly does not obligate immediate action,
but it does invite honesty.
Today invites you to trust what awareness reveals.
Truth is supportive, even when it is challenging.

Affirmation

I trust the clarity that awareness brings.
Truth supports my growth.

Reflection Question

What clarity am I ready to trust right now?

Awareness
Noticing without needing to change

Embodiment Focus
Present-moment awareness
Nervous System Tone: Regulation + clarity

Practice

- Sit or stand comfortably, feet grounded
- Allow your spine to lengthen naturally
- Let your arms rest easily by your sides or in your lap

1. Begin with the senses

- Silently name three things you can see
- Two things you can hear
- One physical sensation you can feel

2. Soften the breath

- Take one slow inhale through the nose
- Exhale gently through the mouth
- Allow the breath to return to its natural rhythm

3. Widen awareness

- Without changing anything, notice:
    - Your body
    - Your emotional state
    - The space around you

- Let everything exist just as it is for 30–60 seconds

When ready, gently re-engage with your surroundings.

Why This Supports Awareness

Awareness begins with noticing, not fixing. This embodiment helps the nervous system shift out of reactivity and into presence, allowing clarity to arise without effort or judgment.

*Awareness does not demand change
it invites understanding.*

Time made visible.

Evaluation

Reflecting without self-criticism

Autumn invites reflection, not as a measure of worth, but as a source of understanding. Evaluation asks you to look back with curiosity rather than regret.

What worked? What didn't? What surprised you? This is not about fixing the past. It is about learning from it.
When evaluation is gentle,
it becomes a guide rather than a weight.

*Reflection becomes wisdom
when compassion leads.*

Evaluation of Body

Reflection

Your body carries the imprint of what you've lived
habits formed, tension released, strength gained.
Today invites you to notice what your body
reveals about this season.
Not as a measure of success or failure,
but as information.
The body reflects experience honestly
and without agenda.

Affirmation

I listen to my body as a source of understanding.

Reflection Question

What does my body reflect about how I've been living?

Evalution of Emotion

Reflection

Evaluation brings emotional insight.
You may notice which emotions linger
and which have softened.
Today invites you to observe emotional patterns
with curiosity rather than blame.
Insight grows when emotions are studied gently.

Affirmation

I observe my emotions with curiosity and care.

Reflection Question

What emotional pattern is becoming clearer?

Evaluation of Choice

Reflection

Evaluation asks you to pause before reacting. Today invites you to choose reflection looking back with perspective instead of responding impulsively. Reflection creates space for wiser choices ahead.

Affirmation

I choose reflection instead of reaction.

Reflection Question

What situation could benefit from thoughtful reflection?

Evaluation of Rest

Reflection

Evaluation often triggers self-criticism.
Today invites you to rest from harsh judgment
and allow understanding to replace blame.
Growth becomes visible
when you soften your inner voice.

Affirmation

I release self-criticism and allow understanding.

Reflection Question

Where can I soften my self-judgment today?

Evaluation of Relationship

Reflection

Autumn reflection clarifies relationships.
You may notice where connection
feels reciprocal and where it feels strained.
Today invites you to evaluate without assigning fault.
Clarity supports healthy recalibration.

Affirmation

I reflect on my relationships with
honesty and compassion.

Reflection Question

What relationship dynamic is becoming clearer?

Evaluation of Perception

Reflection

Evaluation sharpens perception.
Patterns emerge when you look
across time rather than isolated moments.
Today invites you to notice
recurring themeswithout judgment.
Awareness of pattern is the beginning of change.

Affirmation

I see patterns with clarity and neutrality.

Reflection Question

What pattern do I notice repeating?

Evaluation of Trust

Reflection

The purpose of evaluation is insight
not self-punishment.
Today invites you to trust
the understanding that reflection brings.
Insight is a gift that guides future choices with wisdom.

Affirmation

I trust the insights I gain through reflection.
Understanding supports my growth.

Reflection Question

What insight am I ready to trust now?

Evaluation
Seeing clearly without judgment

Embodiment Focus
Neutral observation
Nervous System Tone: Regulation + objectivity

Practice

- Sit or stand comfortably with both feet grounded
- Allow your spine to lengthen, shoulders soft
- Place one hand lightly on your lower abdomen, the other on your chest

1. Settle into the body
- Take a slow inhale through the nose
- Exhale gently through the mouth
- Repeat 2–3 times, allowing the body to settle

2. Create inner distance
- Imagine you are stepping back half a step inside yourself
- From this place, silently observe:
- Your current energy
- Your emotional tone
- Your level of clarity or fatigue

Do not label anything as good or bad — simply notice

3. Name without story
- Silently complete one sentence:
  "What I notice right now is…"

Let the sentence end naturally, without explanation
Remain here for 30–60 seconds, then gently return attention outward.

Why This Supports Evaluation

Evaluation becomes wise when it is separated from judgment. This embodiment helps the nervous system create enough space to assess reality clearly, allowing insight without self-attack or urgency.

Evaluation brings clarity when compassion is present.

Acknowledging what remains.

Gratitude

Honoring what sustained you

As harvest season arrives, gratitude becomes tangible. This is the gratitude of acknowledgment, noticing what nourished you, supported you, or carried you through.

You do not need to feel grateful for everything. Only for what truly mattered. Gratitude allows you to gather nourishment without clinging to it.

What is appreciated can be carried forward.

Gratitude of Body

Reflection

As the season cools,
the body remembers what carried it through,
rest that restored you,
nourishment that strengthened you,
rhythms that steadied you.
Today invites you to notice where your body
feels supported rather than strained.
Gratitude in Autumn is grounded and real.
It honors what worked.

Affirmation

I acknowledge what has supported my body.

Reflection Question

What has physically supported me during this season?

Gratitude of Emotion

Reflection

Gratitude does not require constant positivity.
It asks only that you notice what helped you
feel steady, understood,
or less alone.
Today invites you to recognize emotional supports
inner or outer that carried you when things felt heavy.

Affirmation

I honor the emotional support that sustained me.

Reflection Question

What emotion or inner strength helped me through?

Gratitude of Choice

Reflection

Autumn gratitude is a conscious choice
to acknowledge what contributed to your well-being.
Today invites you to name what helped,
habits, people, moments, or decisions.
Recognition allows nourishment to be integrated.

Affirmation

I choose to acknowledge what sustained me.

Reflection Question

What support am I ready to recognize today?

Gratitude of Rest

Reflection

Gratitude settles when you allow yourself
to rest within it.
Today invites you to pause
and let appreciation soften your nervous system.
Resting in gratitude reinforces stability and ease.

Affirmation

I allow appreciation to bring rest.

Reflection Question

Where can gratitude help me soften today?

Gratitude of Relationship

Reflection

Autumn invites you to notice who showed up
consistently not perfectly, but genuinely.
Today invites you to feel gratitude
for presence, reliability, or shared understanding.
Appreciation deepens connection without expectation.

Affirmation

I appreciate the relationships that supported me.

Reflection Question

Who offered support in a quiet but meaningful way?

Gratitude of Perception

Reflection

Gratitude sharpens perception.
You may begin to see value in experiences
that once felt ordinary or overlooked.
Today invites you to recognize how small,
steady supports made a difference.

Affirmation

I see value in what once went unnoticed.

Reflection Question

What support do I see differently now?

Gratitude of Trust

Reflection

Gratitude becomes complete when you trust that
what sustained you was not accidental.
Today invites you to trust the systems:
internal and external that carried you.
What sustains you deserves confidence and care.

Affirmation

I trust what sustains me.
I carry gratitude forward with wisdom.

Reflection Question

What sustaining support can I trust more deeply?

Gratitude

Receiving what has already been given

Embodiment Focus

Opening to receive
Nervous System Tone: Safety + appreciation

Practice

Sit or stand comfortably with feet grounded
Let your shoulders soften and your jaw relax
Place one or both hands over your heart

1. Ground the body
- Take one slow inhale through the nose
- Exhale gently through the mouth
- Allow the breath to settle naturally

2. Feel rather than list
- Instead of naming things you are grateful for, notice:
- One sensation of warmth, steadiness, or ease in your body
- Or one moment from the day that felt supportive or kind
let the feeling be enough — no need to expand it

3. Receive
- On the next inhale, imagine the body gently opening
- On the exhale, allow that sense of appreciation to settle inward

Remain with this feeling for 30–60 seconds.

Why This Supports Gratitude

Gratitude deepens when it is felt rather than counted. This embodiment helps the nervous system register safety and sufficiency, allowing appreciation to arise naturally instead of being forced.

*Gratitude grows
when we allow ourselves to receive.*

Letting go without force.

Release

Letting go with intention

Autumn is known for release. Leaves fall not because they failed, but because their time has passed.
Release is a natural part of completion.

This theme invites you to let go without resentment or fear. What you release now makes room for rest and renewal later. Nothing needs to be forced.

Release creates space for what comes next

Release of Body

Reflection

As seasons change,
the body naturally releases what it no longer needs,
tension, patterns of holding, habitual bracing.
Today invites you to notice
where your body is ready to soften or exhale.
Release does not require force.
It happens when safety is felt.

Affirmation

I allow my body to release what it no longer needs.

Reflection Question

Where does my body feel ready to soften today?

Release of Emotion

Reflection

Release in Autumn often shows up
as emotional unclenching.
Old disappointments, lingering expectations,
or unspoken grief may surface not to overwhelm you,
but to be freed.
Today invites you to allow feelings to move
through without holding them in place.

Affirmation

I allow emotions to move and release naturally.

Reflection Question

What emotion feels ready to be released?

Release of Choice

Reflection

Release becomes intentional
when you choose not to carry what no longer serves.
Today invites you to notice
one belief, habit, or expectation that feels complete.
Letting go creates space without loss.

Affirmation

I choose to release what is complete.

Reflection Question

What am I choosing not to carry forward?

Release of Rest

Reflection

Release can feel disorienting
if you move too quickly afterward.
Today invites you to rest in the space
created by letting go.
Rest allows the nervous system
to recalibrate and recognize safety.

Affirmation

I allow rest to follow release.

Reflection Question

How can I honor the space created today?

Release of Relationship

Reflection

As seasons change,
roles in relationships may no longer fit.
Today invites you to release outdated expectations
of yourself or others without blame.
Letting go creates room for more honest connection.

Affirmation

I release roles that no longer reflect who I am.

Reflection Question

What relational expectation feels complete?

Release of Perception

Reflection

Release is often mistaken for loss.
Today invites you to see it as completion.
When perception shifts,
letting go feels dignified rather than painful.
What is released has already served its purpose.

Affirmation

I see release as a natural completion.

Reflection Question

How does my view of release change
when I see it as completion?

Release of Trust

Reflection

The final act of release is trust.
Trusting the space that remains.
You do not need to fill it immediately.
Today invites you to trust that emptiness is fertile,
not lacking.
What is meant to grow will find room.

Affirmation

I trust the space created by release.
What is meant to come will come.

Reflection Question

What would it feel like to trust the space I've created?

Release

Letting go without urgency

Embodiment Focus

Gentle letting go
Nervous System Tone: Safety + relief

Practice

- Stand or sit comfortably with both feet grounded
- Allow your arms to hang loosely by your sides
- Let your gaze soften or close your eyes

1. Gather
- Inhale slowly through the nose
- As you inhale, gently curl your hands into soft fists
- Imagine gathering what you have been holding
  thoughts, effort, emotion

2. Release
- Exhale slowly through the mouth
- As you exhale, open your hands and let your arms soften
- Imagine placing down what no longer needs to be carried

3. Pause
- Rest with hands open for a few breaths
- Notice any shift in sensation:
   warmth, space, ease, or neutrality

Repeat 3–5 times, moving slowly and without force.

Why This Supports Release

Release happens through safety, not pressure. This embodiment teaches the body that letting go does not mean loss — it means relief. When the nervous system feels supported, release becomes natural.

What is released creates space for what is next.

What remains when excess falls away.

Simplification

Choosing less with clarity

As the season shifts, excess becomes apparent.
Simplification is not deprivation, it is refinement.
It asks what truly deserves your energy now.

In Autumn, choosing less allows what remains to feel more meaningful. Simplification restores focus and ease.

Less can be a form of care.

Simplification of Body

Reflection

When life simplifies,
the body often responds with relief.
Breathing deepens.
Tension softens.
Movement becomes more fluid.
Today invites you to notice where your body
feels lighter when excess is removed.
Simplicity supports physical ease.

Affirmation

I allow my body to experience ease
through simplicity.

Reflection Question

What feels lighter in my body when I do less today?

Simplification of Emotion

Reflection

Simplification eases emotional load. When you stop carrying what is unnecessary, feelings have more room to move naturally. Today invites you to notice which emotional responsibilities can be set down without guilt.

Affirmation

I release emotional weight that is not mine to carry.

Reflection Question

What emotional weight can I set down today?

Simplification of Choice

Reflection

Simplification is an intentional choice.
Today invites you to choose what truly matters
and let go of what distracts.
Fewer commitments, clearer priorities,
and intentional focus create steadiness.

Affirmation

I choose what matters most with clarity.

Reflection Question

What deserves my attention more
than everything else right now?

Simplification of Rest

Reflection

Rest deepens when life feels uncluttered.
Today invites you to rest in the space
created by simplicity
allowing quiet to restore rather than unsettle you.
Less creates room for renewal.

Affirmation

I rest comfortably in simplicity.

Reflection Question

Where can I enjoy the quiet created by doing less?

Simplification of Relationship

Reflection

Simplification in relationship invites honesty.
Today invites you to notice which connections
feel reciprocal and which feel draining.
Simplifying does not mean withdrawing
it means relating with clarity and intention.

Affirmation

I simplify my relationships with honesty and care.

Reflection Question

Where can clarity improve a relationship right now?

Simplification of Perception

Reflection

Simplification sharpens perception.
When distractions fade, essentials stand out.
Today invites you to see what truly supports your well-being
without needing to justify your choices.

Affirmation

I see clearly what is essential.

Reflection Question

What feels essential now that once felt optional?

Simplification of Trust

Reflection

Trusting simplicity means believing
that less can be enough.
Today invites you to trust that reducing complexity
supports depth rather than diminishes possibility.
Simplicity creates strength.

Affirmation

I trust simplicity to support my life.
Less creates clarity and ease.

Reflection Question

What would change if I trusted simplicity fully?

Simplification

Returning to what is essential

Embodiment Focus

Clarity through reduction
Nervous System Tone: Regulation + ease

Practice

- Sit or stand comfortably with feet grounded
- Let your shoulders drop and your breath soften
- Place one hand on your lower abdomen, the other on your chest

1. Exhale first
- Take a slow exhale through the mouth
- Let the inhale come naturally afterward
- Repeat 2–3 times, allowing the body to settle

2. Remove, don't add
- With each exhale, imagine gently removing one layer:
    - A thought
    - An expectation
    - A task or obligation
- Do not replace it with anything, simply create space

3. Rest in what remains
- Pause for 30–60 seconds
- Notice the simplicity of breath, body, and presence
- When ready, return attention to your surroundings.

Why This Supports Simplification

Simplification restores clarity by reducing input rather than increasing effort. This embodiment helps the nervous system release excess stimulation, allowing what matters to stand out naturally.

Simplicity reveals what was already enough.

Knowledge gathered through experience.

Wisdom

Learning from lived experience

Wisdom grows from experience that has been reflected upon.
Autumn wisdom is earned, not taught. It lives quietly in what you now understand without
 explanation.

You may notice a deeper trust in your discernment or a softer response to situations that once felt charged.
This is growth integrated.

Wisdom is experience made gentle

Wisdom of Body

Reflection

Your body remembers what your mind may forget.
It carries lessons learned
through repetition, recovery, and resilience.
Today invites you to notice how your body
responds differently than it once did
perhaps with quicker recovery, clearer signals,
or steadier pacing.
Wisdom lives in what the body
no longer needs to be taught.

Affirmation

My body carries wisdom from all I've lived.

Reflection Question

What does my body know now that it didn't before?

Wisdom of Emotion

Reflection

Wisdom shows up emotionally as steadiness.
Feelings still arise,
but they pass with less intensity or confusion.
Today invites you to notice how emotions
move through you now
what no longer hooks you the way it once did.
Emotional wisdom creates spaciousness.

Affirmation

I meet my emotions with maturity and ease.

Reflection Question

Which emotion feels easier to navigate now?

Wisdom of Choice

Reflection

Wisdom informs choice.
You no longer decide only from hope or fear,
but from experience.
Today invites you to notice how past lessons
guide present decisions.
Choosing wisely is often quieter than choosing quickly.

Affirmation

I choose from experience and understanding.

Reflection Question

What experience is guiding a choice I'm making now?

Wisdom of Rest

Reflection

Wisdom allows rest from constant learning.
You do not need to keep seeking
answers you already hold.
Today invites you to rest in what you know
trusting that understanding is already integrated.

Affirmation

I rest in the wisdom I already carry.

Reflection Question

What do I no longer need to question?

Wisdom of Relationship

Reflection

Wisdom in relationship brings discernment.
You may notice clearer boundaries,
healthier patterns, or deeper compassion.
Today invites you to observe how wisdom
shows up in the way you relate
without needing to explain or correct.

Affirmation

I relate with wisdom and respect.

Reflection Question

How has wisdom changed the way
I connect with others?

Wisdom of Perception

Reflection

Wisdom widens perspective.
You see situations within a larger context,
less reactive, more measured.
Today invites you to notice how your perception
has expanded through experience.
Seeing broadly creates calm.

Affirmation

I see life through the lens of understanding.

Reflection Question

Where do I see more clearly than I once did?

Wisdom of Trust

Reflection

The final step of wisdom is trust.
Trust in insight that has been earned, not borrowed.
Today invites you to trust what you
know without second-guessing.
Wisdom is quiet confidence grounded in lived truth.

Affirmation

I trust the wisdom I have earned.
My experience guides me well.

Reflection Question

What insight am I ready to trust completely?

Wisdom
Listening to what already knows

Embodiment Focus

Inner knowing
Nervous System Tone: Regulation + coherence

Practice

- Sit or stand comfortably with feet grounded
- Lengthen the spine gently, without effort
- Place one hand on your heart and one on your lower abdomen

1. Settle the body
- Take a slow inhale through the nose
- Exhale softly through the mouth
- Repeat 2–3 times, allowing the body to become steady

2. Listen inward
- Bring attention to the space beneath your thoughts
- Without asking a question, notice:
   - Sensations
   - Images
   - A felt sense of "yes," "no," or neutrality
- Let whatever arises be enough

3. Anchor the knowing
- On the next exhale, gently press your feet into the ground
- Feel the steadiness of being supported

Remain here for 30–60 seconds, then slowly return awareness outward.

Why This Supports Wisdom

Wisdom emerges when the nervous system is calm enough to listen. This embodiment quiets mental noise and strengthens trust in subtle inner signals that arise from experience rather than analysis.

Wisdom does not rush, it reveals itself when we listen.

Structure shaped with care.

Deliberate Boundaries

Protecting what matters.

Boundaries in Autumn are deliberate. They help preserve energy as the season slows. This is about choosing what you allow in and what you no longer do.

Boundaries are not rejection. They are stewardship of your inner resources.

Protection allows preservation.

Deliberate Boundaries of Body

Reflection

As the season cools,
the body naturally signals its limits.
You may notice a need
for more rest, warmth, or steadier rhythms.
Today invites you to listen without resistance.
Boundaries in the body are not restrictions
they are guidance for preservation.

Affirmation

I honor my body's limits as wisdom.

Reflection Question

What limit is my body asking me to respect today?

Deliberate Boundaries of Emotion

Reflection

Autumn boundaries include emotional containment the ability to feel without becoming overwhelmed. Today invites you to notice where you need to hold emotions gently rather than spill them everywhere. Containment creates safety and clarity.

Affirmation

I hold my emotions with care and respect.

Reflection Question

What emotion needs gentle containment right now?

Deliberate Boundaries of Choice

Reflection

Boundaries are chosen, not imposed.
Today invites you to notice where you are
allowing too much or too little.
Choosing boundaries consciously protects
your energy and attention.
What you allow shapes your inner environment.

Affirmation

I choose what I allow with intention.

Reflection Question

What do I need to allow or not allow today?

Deliberate Boundaries of Rest

Reflection

Boundaries create rest by reducing demand.
Today invites you to rest behind
the boundaries you've set
trusting that stepping back does not mean disengaging.
Rest restores strength.

Affirmation

I rest comfortably within my boundaries.

Reflection Question

How does rest feel when my boundaries are respected

Deliberate Boundaries of Relationship

Reflection

Autumn boundaries clarify relationships.
You may find it easier to say no,
to ask for space,
or to be honest about capacity.
Today invites you to honor
relational boundaries without guilt.
Clear boundaries allow connection to remain healthy.

Affirmation

I honor boundaries in my relationships.

Reflection Question

What boundary supports a relationship right now?

Deliberate Boundaries of Perception

Reflection

Boundaries are often misinterpreted as distance.
Today invites you to see them
as care for yourself and others.
When perception shifts, boundaries feel
supportive rather than defensive.

Affirmation

I see boundaries as acts of care.

Reflection Question

How does my view of boundaries change
when I see them as care?

Deliberate Boundaries of Trust

Reflection

Trust in Autumn means trusting yourself
to protect what matters without over-explaining.
Today invites you to trust your judgment
and your right to preserve energy, time, and truth.
Stewardship is an act of self-respect.

Affirmation

I trust myself to protect what matters most.
My boundaries are wise and necessary.

Reflection Question

What am I ready to protect more intentionally?

Deliberate Boundaries
Choosing what is allowed to enter and remain

Embodiment Focus
Self-containment + choice
Nervous System Tone: Safety + agency

Practice

- Stand or sit comfortably with both feet grounded
- Lengthen the spine gently
- Let your arms rest by your sides

1. Establish your space

- Slowly raise your hands in front of you, palms facing inward
- Bring them about shoulder-width apart, as if outlining your personal space
- Take one steady breath here

2. Clarify the boundary

- On an inhale, gently draw your elbows slightly inward toward your ribs
- On the exhale, extend your forearms forward a few inches, palms open

- This motion signals choice, not pushing away

3. Anchor the decision

Lower your arms and press your feet lightly into the ground

Notice the feeling of containment, steadiness, and clarity

Repeat 2–3 times, moving slowly and intentionally.

Why This Supports Deliberate Boundaries

Boundaries become sustainable when they are embodied rather than enforced. This practice helps the nervous system feel safe within chosen limits, reinforcing that boundaries are an act of self-respect, not separation.

Boundaries protect what matters.

Tending what has been chosen.

Responsibility

Owning your choices with integrity.

Autumn responsibility is grounded and calm. It is the recognition that you are shaping your life through what you choose to carry forward.

This theme invites ownership without blame. Responsibility empowers you to move forward with clarity.

Ownership strengthens agency.

Responsibility of Body

Reflection

The body relaxes when responsibility is claimed honestly. Tension often arises not from responsibility itself, but from avoidance or over-carrying what is not yours. Today invites you to notice how your body feels when you own what is truly yours and set down what is not.

Affirmation

I allow my body to relax into honest responsibility.

Reflection Question

What feels lighter when I own what is truly mine?

Responsibility of Emotion

Reflection

Responsibility does not mean suppressing emotion.
It means recognizing what belongs to you
emotionally and what does not.
Today invites you to own your feelings
without projecting them onto others or circumstances.
Emotional responsibility brings clarity and steadiness.

Affirmation

I take responsibility for my emotions with compassion.

Reflection Question

What feeling am I ready to own without blame?

Responsibility of Choice

Reflection

Responsibility is agency in action.
Today invites you to recognize where
you have choice even if options feel limited.
Ownership empowers movement.
When you choose agency,
you step out of passivity and into authorship.

Affirmation

I choose agency over avoidance.

Reflection Question

Where do I have more choice than I realize?

Responsibility of Rest

Reflection

True responsibility includes rest.
Over-responsibility exhausts and blurs clarity.
Today invites you to rest from carrying
what is not yours to fix or manage.
Stepping back is often the most responsible act.

Affirmation

I release responsibility that is not mine.

Reflection Question

What can I stop carrying today?

Responsibility of Relationship

Reflection

Healthy relationships thrive on shared responsibility.
Today invites you to notice where you are taking
too much responsibility or too little.
Owning your part creates balance and respect.

Affirmation

I own my part in relationships with honesty.

Reflection Question

What is my responsibility and what is not
in a relationship right now?

Responsibility of Perception

Reflection

Responsibility is often distorted by guilt or obligation.
Today invites you to see it clearly,
as empowerment rather than burden.
When perception shifts,
responsibility feels stabilizing instead of heavy.

Affirmation

I see responsibility as a source of strength.

Reflection Question

How does responsibility feel when
I see it as empowerment?

Responsibility of Trust

Reflection

The final act of responsibility is trust.
Trusting yourself to lead your life with integrity.
You do not need perfection to be responsible.
You only need honesty and presence.

Affirmation

I trust myself to lead my life wisely.
I stand in responsible ownership.

Reflection Question

What would change if I trusted myself to lead fully?

Responsibility

Owning what is yours to carry

Embodiment Focus

Grounded ownership
Nervous System Tone: Stability + self-trust

Practice

- Stand or sit comfortably with both feet grounded
- Allow your spine to rise naturally, shoulders relaxed
- Place one hand over your heart and one hand over your lower abdomen

1. Claim your center
- Take a slow inhale through the nose
- Feel the support beneath your feet and seat
- Exhale gently, allowing your weight to settle downward

2. Separate what is yours
- On the next breath, silently note:
    - What is mine to tend
    - What is not mine to carry
- Let this be felt rather than analyzed

3. Anchor ownership
- Gently press your feet into the ground

- Feel the steadiness of standing in your role without overreaching

Remain here for 30–60 seconds, breathing naturally.

Why This Supports Responsibility

True responsibility is grounded, not heavy. This embodiment helps the nervous system distinguish between healthy ownership and unnecessary burden, reinforcing confidence, clarity, and self-respect.

Responsibility strengthens when it is carried with clarity.

Standing true through seasons

Integrity

Aligning actions with truth.

Integrity is the alignment between what you know and how you live. In Autumn, integrity becomes more visible. What feels true stands out.

This season invites you to make small adjustments that bring your life into greater coherence. Integrity simplifies decision-making.

Alignment creates steadiness.

Integrity of Body

Reflection

Integrity is felt in the body as ease.
When actions align with truth,
the body softens rather than braces.
Today invites you to notice
where your body feels relaxed and where it tightens.
These sensations offer guidance without words.

Affirmation

I listen to my body as a guide to alignment.

Reflection Question

Where does my body feel most at ease today?

Integrity of Emotion

Reflection

Emotional integrity arises when feelings
and actions are not at odds.
Today invites you to notice where emotions
are honored rather than overridden.
When you allow feelings to inform your choices,
inner conflict lessens.

Affirmation

I honor my emotions as part of my truth.

Reflection Question

Where am I feeling emotionally aligned or misaligned?

Integrity of Choice

Reflection

Integrity is practiced through choice.
Today invites you to choose actions that reflect
what you value, even when they are quiet or unseen.
Small choices made in alignment
create deep trust within yourself.

Affirmation

I choose actions that reflect my values.

Reflection Question

What choice today reflects what matters most to me?

Integrity of Rest

Reflection

When integrity is present, inner conflict eases.
Today invites you to rest from self-negotiation
and allow clarity to guide you.
Rest restores energy when choices
no longer pull you in opposite directions.

Affirmation

I allow rest to come from inner alignment.

Reflection Question

Where can I stop negotiating against myself?

Integrity in Relationship

Reflection

Integrity in relationship means being honest without being harsh.
Today invites you to notice where you can show up more truthfully while remaining respectful.
Alignment strengthens trust.

Affirmation

I relate with honesty and care.

Reflection Question

Where can I bring more truth into a relationship?

Integrity of Perception

Reflection

Integrity clarifies perception.
You begin to see yourself not as who you should be,
but as who you are.
Today invites you to view yourself
with honesty and compassion.
Clear seeing builds self-respect.

Affirmation

I see myself clearly and kindly.

Reflection Question

What truth about myself am I ready to acknowledge?

Integrity of Trust

Reflection

The final act of integrity is trust.
Trust that living in alignment will guide you forward.
You may not see immediate outcomes,
but alignment creates stability over time.
Today invites you to trust the path that feels true.

Affirmation

I trust the power of living in alignment.
My truth guides me.

Reflection Question

What does trusting alignment feel like right now?

Integrity

Living in alignment with what is true

Embodiment Focus

Inner alignment
Nervous System Tone: Coherence + steadiness

Practice

- Stand or sit comfortably with both feet grounded
- Allow your spine to lengthen naturally
- Place one hand over your heart and one hand over your lower abdomen

1. Align vertically
- Take a slow inhale through the nose
- Imagine the breath moving from your feet to the crown of your head
- Exhale slowly, allowing the body to settle into alignment

2. Check for congruence
- Silently notice:
- What feels true in your body
- Where there may be tension or hesitation
- Do not adjust — simply observe

3. Anchor truth
- Gently press your feet into the ground
- Allow the body to organize itself around what feels honest

Remain here for 30–60 seconds, breathing naturally.

Why This Supports Integrity

Integrity is embodied when the nervous system senses coherence between inner truth and outward action. This practice strengthens that felt sense of alignment, making it easier to act from honesty rather than obligation.

Integrity is felt before it is spoken.

Saving what will sustain.

Preservation

Saving what sustains you.

Autumn teaches preservation, storing nourishment for the seasons ahead. This theme is about recognizing what supports you and ensuring it remains accessible.

Preservation is an act of foresight and care.

What you preserve sustains you later.

Preservation of Body

Reflection

As light fades and temperatures cool,
the body naturally conserves energy.
Today invites you to honor this instinct,
slower movement, warmer nourishment,
steadier pacing.
Preservation in the body is wisdom
preparing you for rest, not weakness.

Affirmation

I honor my body's need to conserve and care for energy.

Reflection Question

What does my body need to conserve today?

Preservation of Emotion

Reflection

Preservation includes protecting emotional reserves.
Today invites you to notice where
you can be gentler with your feelings
limiting exposure to what drains you
and staying close to what steadies you.
Emotional safekeeping creates resilience.

Affirmation

I protect my emotional energy with care.

Reflection Question

What emotional boundary helps me
feel steady right now?

Preservation of Choice

Reflection

Preservation asks you to choose
what is worth maintaining.
Not everything needs
improvement or expansion.
Today invites you to commit to what already
works: habits, relationships, or rhythms
that support your well-being.

Affirmation

I choose to maintain what sustains me.

Reflection Question

What is worth preserving as it is?

Preservation of Rest

Reflection

Rest is an act of preservation.
Today invites you to rest before depletion
not as escape, but as stewardship.
Strength is protected when rest is intentional.

Affirmation

I rest to preserve my strength.

Reflection Question

How can rest support me today?

Preservation of Relationship

Reflection

Preservation in relationship focuses on steadiness rather than intensity.
Today invites you to nurture reliable connections, those that feel grounding and safe.
Preservation honors continuity over excitement.

Affirmation

I preserve relationships that provide steadiness.

Reflection Question

Which connection feels worth tending gently?

Preservation of Perception

Reflection

Preservation sharpens perception.
You begin to see what truly matters
when excess has fallen away.
Today invites you to recognize what deserves
protection, time, energy, values, or peace.

Affirmation

I see clearly what is worth keeping.

Reflection Question

What feels essential to protect now?

Preservation of Trust

Reflection

Preservation requires trust.
Trust that caring for what sustains you is enough.
You do not need constant growth to be moving forward.
Today invites you to trust stewardship as progress.

Affirmation

I trust stewardship as a form of growth.
What I protect continues.

Reflection Question

What would it feel like to trust preservation fully?

Preservation
Protecting what is essential

Embodiment Focus

Conservation + care
Nervous System Tone: Safety + sustainability

Practice

- Sit or stand comfortably with both feet grounded
- Allow your shoulders to soften and your breath to slow
- Bring your hands gently toward your center

1. Gather inward
- On a slow inhale, draw your hands toward your chest or abdomen
- Imagine gathering what is precious — energy, clarity, intention
- Keep the movement gentle, not tight

2. Contain with care
- On the exhale, rest your hands over your heart or lower abdomen
- Feel the sense of holding without gripping
- Allow the body to register safety

3. Stabilize
- Take 2–3 natural breaths
- Feel your feet, your weight, and the steadiness of being supported

Remain here for 30–60 seconds, breathing comfortably.

Why This Supports Preservation

Preservation is not fear-based protection, it is wise stewardship. This embodiment teaches the nervous system how to conserve energy and protect what matters without closing off
or hardening.

What is preserved with care remains alive.

Essence revealed as clarity.

Distillation

Refining what truly matters

Distillation is the art of refinement.

Autumn teaches us that wisdom does not come from holding everything. It comes from discerning what is essential. Experiences, lessons, relationships, and efforts begin to clarify. What once felt tangled starts to simplify.

Distillation is not loss.
It is concentration.

In this season, life asks what is worth carrying forward and what can be gently laid down. Energy is preserved. Meaning deepens. What remains is lighter, clearer, and more aligned.

Here, you are not becoming less.

You are becoming more precise

Distillation of Body

Reflection

The body begins to signal what is essential
and what is excess.
Energy naturally conserves.
Movement becomes more intentional.
The body asks to carry only what is necessary.

Affirmation

I listen to what my body truly needs.

Reflection Question

What does my body feel ready to simplify or release?

Distillation of Emotion

Reflection

As the season turns, emotions clarify.
What once felt loud softens into something more honest.
Distillation allows feeling to settle into truth
rather than reaction.

Affirmation

I allow my emotions to clarify naturally.

Reflection Question

Which feelings feel essential and which feel complete?

Distillation of Choice

Reflection

Autumn refines decision-making.
Choices are no longer driven by possibility alone,
but by alignment.
Distillation asks which paths deserve continued energy.

Affirmation

I choose what truly matters.

Reflection Question

What choice feels ready to be simplified or concluded?

Distillation of Rest

Reflection

Rest becomes discerning rather than indulgent.
It restores by removing excess stimulation
and unnecessary effort.
Distilled rest nourishes deeply.

Affirmation

I rest in ways that truly restore me.

Reflection Question

What form of rest feels most nourishing right now?

Distillation of Relationship

Reflection

Relationships clarify in Autumn.
Some deepen through authenticity;
others gently complete.
Distillation honors connection
without forcing continuation.

Affirmation

I honor relationships that feel true and aligned.

Reflection Question

Which connections feel essential
and which feel complete?

Distillation of Perception

Reflection

Perspective sharpens when distractions fall away.
Distillation allows truth to emerge
without embellishment, urgency, or defense.

Affirmation

I see my life with clarity and honesty.

Reflection Question

What feels clearer now than it did before?

Distillation of Trust

Reflection

Trust deepens when we stop carrying
what no longer belongs to us.
Distillation reinforces confidence in what remains.

Affirmation

I trust what remains after refinement.

Reflection Question

What do I trust more deeply now that I've simplified?

Distillation
Refining until only what matters remains

Embodiment Focus
Essence + clarity
Nervous System Tone: Regulation + coherence

Practice

- Sit or stand comfortably with both feet grounded
- Let your shoulders soften and your jaw relax

Place one hand on your heart, one hand on your lower abdomen

1. Settle the field
- Take a slow inhale through the nose
- Exhale gently through the mouth
- With each breath, imagine excess noise or effort settling downward

2. Refine

- On the next few breaths, silently ask:
- What is essential right now?
- Do not search for an answer

Simply notice what remains present when everything else quiets

3. Anchor what remains
- Gently press your feet into the ground
- Allow your spine to organize around what feels steady and true

Remain here for 30–60 seconds, breathing naturally.

Why This Supports Distillation

Distillation happens through reduction, not addition. This embodiment helps the nervous system quiet competing inputs so clarity can arise naturally. What remains is not forced, it is revealed.

When the unnecessary falls away, truth becomes simple.

The Threshold from Autumn to Winter

A turning inward

Autumn teaches us how to let go with intention.
Winter teaches us how to rest without guilt.

As the outer world quiets, what remains becomes clearer.
What was gathered has been refined.
What was essential has been kept. Now, even that can be set down.

The transition into Winter is not
a loss of momentum,
it is a return to depth.

Here, the work is no longer visible. Growth moves beneath the surface. Effort gives way to presence. Understanding softens into acceptance.

You are not meant to carry everything forward.
You are not meant to keep deciding.

This threshold invites you to release the need to evaluate, improve, or prepare. What matters has already been distilled. What remains will be held by stillness.

As you cross into Winter, allow yourself to slow.
Allow questions to remain unanswered.
Allow rest to become meaningful.

Nothing is being asked of you now.

The Threshold from Autumn to Winter

Reflection Questions

What am I ready to stop carrying?

What no longer needs my attention?

Where do I feel called to rest rather than respond?

*Winter begins when you allow yourself
to lay things down
not because they failed,
but because they are complete.*

Winter

Stillness & Remembrance

The Season of Being

Winter is the season of stillness. It is a time of rest, incubation, and quiet renewal. What appears dormant is not gone.
 it is integrating, restoring, and remembering itself beneath the surface.

This season invites you to step out of striving and into presence. Winter teaches that you are not defined by movement or productivity. It is here that essence becomes visible.
The part of you that remains constant through every change.

Throughout this chapter, you will move through themes of stillness, rest, incubation, reflection, acceptance, surrender, faith, grace, renewal, hope, emergence, and divine essence. Together, these themes offer a return to being before the next beginning unfolds.

Winter does not ask you to prepare.
It asks you to remember who you are.

*Nothing moves,
yet everything is held.*

Stillness

The quiet that holds everything

Stillness is not empty.
It is full of listening.

In a world that praises motion, Winter reminds us that life continues even when we stop moving. Beneath the surface, breath slows, attention softens, and what matters most begins to speak more clearly.

Stillness is where the noise settles.
It is where truth no longer has to compete.

This season does not ask you to withdraw from life, but to rest inside it , to notice what remains when striving quiets and effort loosens its grip. In stillness, nothing needs to be fixed, improved, or explained.

Here, you are allowed to simply be.

Stillness of the Body

Reflection

The body carries wisdom that movement
can sometimes drown out.
In stillness, subtle sensations return:
breath, weight, warmth, and ease.
The body remembers how to be without performing.

Affirmation

My body is allowed to be still.

Reflection Question

What does my body notice when
I stop trying to move or fix it?

Stillness of Emotion

Reflection

Emotions do not disappear in stillness.
they settle.
Without motion or distraction,
feelings soften into something more honest
and less reactive.

Affirmation

I allow my emotions to rest without judgment.

Reflection Question

What emotion becomes quieter
when I stop engaging it?

Stillness of Choice

Reflection

Not every moment requires a decision.
Stillness offers relief from constant choosing,
reminding us that clarity often arrives when we pause.

Affirmation

I do not need to decide everything right now.

Reflection Question

What choice can I allow to wait?

Stillness of Rest

Reflection

Rest deepens when it is free from intention.
Stillness allows rest to move beyond sleep
into true restoration, a settling of the whole system.

Affirmation

I allow rest to be simple.

Reflection Question

What happens when I rest without
trying to recover or prepare?

Stillness of Relationship

Reflection

Stillness creates space to be with others without performing, explaining, or fixing. Presence becomes enough.

Affirmation

I am allowed to be with others in quiet presence.

Reflection Question

What shifts in my relationships when I don't try to manage the moment?

Stillness of Perspective

Reflection

When movement slows, perspective widens. Stillness removes urgency a
nd reveals what matters without distortion.

Affirmation

I allow clarity to come without force.

Reflection Question

What looks different when I step out of urgency?

Stillness of Trust

Reflection

Trust deepens in stillness because it removes control.
In the absence of action,
faith becomes embodied rather than imagined.

Affirmation

I trust life to continue even in stillness.

Reflection Question

What continues to hold me when I do nothing?

Stillness
Resting without needing to move

Embodiment Focus
Deep presence
Nervous System Tone: Safety + settling

Practice

- Sit or lie down comfortably
- Allow your spine to be supported, chair, floor, or wall
- Let your hands rest naturally on your body or beside you

1. Arrive
- Take a slow inhale through the nose
- Exhale gently through the mouth
- Allow the breath to become quiet and unforced

2. Soften the body
- Bring attention to three areas:
    - Jaw
    - Shoulders
    - Belly
- Without changing them, allow each area to soften slightly

3. Rest in presence
- Let your attention widen
- Notice:
    - The weight of your body
    - The support beneath you
    - The space around you

Remain here for 60–90 seconds, doing nothing else
When ready, gently open your eyes or bring awareness back to the room.

Why This Supports Stillness

Stillness is not the absence of life, it is where life settles. This embodiment signals safety to the nervous system, allowing tension to release and awareness to deepen without effort.

Stillness is not emptiness,
it is fullness without motion.

Life paused, not gone.

Rest

Restoring what has been used.

The permission to restore
Rest is not the absence of effort
it is the return of balance.

Winter teaches that restoration is not something to earn.
It arrives when we allow the body to soften and the mind to
release its grip on doing. In rest, energy is not lost;
it is gathered.

Rest is where the nervous system remembers safety.
It is where the body repairs what the seasons have asked of it.

Here, you are allowed to stop.
Rest allows strength to return.

Rest of Body

Reflection

Rest allows the body to repair and replenish quietly.
Muscles soften, breath deepens,
and energy is restored beneath the surface.
Today invites you to notice what kind of rest feels
most supportive, not indulgent, not earned, just necessary.
The body knows how to restore itself
when given permission.

Affirmation

I allow my body to replenish through rest.

Reflection Question

What kind of rest does my body truly need today?

Rest of Emotion

Reflection

Emotions recover through rest as well.
When you stop revisiting or replaying experiences,
emotional energy settles.
Today invites you to give your feelings a break.
to let them rest without analysis.
Emotional recovery happens naturally in quiet.

Affirmation

I allow my emotions to recover through rest.

Reflection Question

What feeling could benefit from being left alone today?

Rest of Choice

Reflection

Rest becomes powerful when it is chosen
rather than postponed.
Today invites you to choose restoration
over productivity or obligation.
Choosing rest is not avoidance,
it is stewardship of your energy.

Affirmation

I choose restoration with intention.

Reflection Question

Where can I choose rest instead of pushing today?

Rest of Rest

Reflection

Deep rest is unstructured and uninterrupted.
Today invites you to rest in ways that disconnect you
from demand, sleep, stillness, warmth, or silence.
Deep rest restores more than energy;
it restores trust in yourself.

Affirmation

I allow myself deep, uninterrupted rest.

Reflection Question

What supports deep rest for me right now?

Rest of Relationship

Reflection

Winter relationships thrive on gentleness.
Today invites you to allow connection
without expectation, no fixing, no processing,
and no problem-solving.
Gentle presence allows rest to be shared.

Affirmation

I allow relationships to be gentle and restful.

Reflection Question

Who feels safe to be gentle with right now?

Rest of Perception

Reflection

Rest is often underestimated.
Today invites you to see rest
as active repair rather than inactivity.
What is restored through rest
cannot be forced through effort.

Affirmation

I see rest as essential repair.

Reflection Question

How does my perception of rest
change when I see it as repair?

Rest of Trust

Reflection

The final act of Winter rest is trust
Trusting that restoration happens
even when you cannot see it.
Today invites you to trust your body, mind,
and spirit to restore themselves when given time and care.

Affirmation

I trust restoration to unfold naturally.
Rest renews me.

Reflection Question

What would change if I trusted rest completely?

Rest
Allowing restoration without effort

Embodiment Focus
Restoration
Nervous System Tone: Safety + replenishment

Practice

- Sit or lie down in a position that feels supportive
- Allow your body to be held by the surface beneath you
Let your hands rest comfortably on your body or beside you

1. Exhale first
- Slowly exhale through the mouth
- Let the inhale come naturally afterward
- Repeat 2-3 times, allowing the body to sink downward

2. Signal permission
- Silently tell your body:
- You are allowed to rest.
- Notice any areas that soften in response

3. Receive support
- Bring attention to:
- Where your body is being supported
- Where weight is being held for you
- Stay here for 1-2 minutes, breathing naturally
When ready, gently re-engage with your surroundings.

Why This Supports Rest

True rest occurs when the nervous system feels safe enough to stop guarding. This embodiment shifts the body out of effort and into restoration, allowing replenishment without pressure or expectation.

*Rest is not a pause from life,
it is life restoring itself.*

What is becoming is protected.

Incubation

What grows unseen

Not everything is meant to be visible yet.

Winter holds what is forming beneath the surface: ideas, healing, and new directions that require darkness and time. Incubation is the season of becoming without announcement.

Nothing is delayed here.
Everything is ripening in its own rhythm.

Trust what is growing quietly.

Incubation of Body

Reflection

Even in stillness,
the body is active beneath the surface.
Cells repair.
Strength gathers.
Energy reorganizes.
Today invites you to trust that your body
is preparing in ways you do not need to manage.
Incubation is happening quietly.

Affirmation

My body prepares in stillness.

Reflection Question

What feels quietly supported in my body right now?

Incubation of Emotion

Reflection

Emotions also incubate.
Feelings you once needed to process
may now be settling into understanding.
Today invites you to let emotions rest
without forcing clarity.
Emotional gestation leads to wisdom without effort.

Affirmation

I allow emotions to gestate without pressure.

Reflection Question

What feeling feels less urgent than it once did?

Incubation of Choice

Reflection

Incubation requires restraint.
Today invites you to choose patience over action.
You are allowed to let ideas, decisions,
and insights mature internally before sharing them.
What is not ready does not need to be pushed.

Affirmation

I choose patience and allow timing to guide me.

Reflection Question

What can I allow more time to develop?

Incubation of Rest

Reflection

Incubation blends rest and becoming.
Today invites you to rest
without worrying that you are falling behind.
Becoming does not require visible effort.
It unfolds in quiet.

Affirmation

I rest while becoming who I am next.

Reflection Question

Where can I rest without concern today?

Incubation of Relationship

Reflection

Some connections are meant to
remain private during incubation.
Today invites you to honor
quiet bonds and internal conversations.
Not everything needs an audience.

Affirmation

I honor what is meant to remain private.

Reflection Question

What feels better kept close right now?

Incubation of Perception

Reflection

Incubation changes perception.
You may sense growth without evidence.
Today invites you to trust what you feel
forming beneath the surface.
Growth does not announce itself until it is ready.

Affirmation

I trust what is forming beneath the surface.

Reflection Question

What growth do I sense but cannot yet name?

Incubation of Trust

Reflection

The final act of incubation is trus,
trusting what you cannot yet see.
Today invites you to trust the unseen
work happening within you.
Timing is intelligence.

Affirmation

I trust the unseen process of becoming.
What is forming will emerge in time.

Reflection Question

What would it feel like to fully trust
what is unfolding unseen?

Incubation

Allowing what is forming to mature unseen

Embodiment Focus
Inner holding + patience
Nervous System Tone: Safety + trust

Practice

- Sit or lie down comfortably
- Allow your body to be fully supported
- Place one or both hands over your lower abdomen or heart

1. Create containment
- Take a slow inhale through the nose
- Feel your hands gently resting on your body
- Exhale softly through the mouth, allowing the body to settle inward

2. Honor the unseen
- Silently acknowledge:
- Something is forming, even if I cannot see it yet.
- Let this be a statement, not a question

3. Rest in patience
- Allow your breath to move naturally
- Imagine warmth or softness surrounding what is forming within you
- Remain here for 1–2 minutes, without trying to define or name anything
When ready, gently return awareness to the room.

Why This Supports Incubation

Incubation requires safety and time. This embodiment reassures the nervous system that growth does not need visibility to be real, allowing patience, trust, and internal maturation to unfold naturally.

What is meant to grow does not need to hurry.

Clarity found in quiet.

Reflection

Seeing clearly, without judgment

Reflection is not about revisiting the past to relive it.
It is about looking back with honesty and compassion.

Winter offers a mirror that does not distort. In reflection,
lessons rise gently, without accusation or urgency.
What matters becomes simpler.
What no longer serves reveals itself without force.

*Clarity comes when we
stop rushing to understand.*

Reflection of Body

Reflection

As activity slows,
the body remembers what has been lived.
Sensations, rhythms, and responses
carry memory without narrative.
Today invites you to notice how your body
holds experience:
Not as story, but as knowing.

Affirmation

My body holds wisdom from all I've lived.

Reflection Question

What does my body remember without words?

Reflection of Emotion

Reflection

Reflection allows emotions to reveal
meaning without force.
Today invites you to notice how feelings
have shifted over time.
What no longer feels charged and what feels settled.
Meaning emerges when emotions are allowed
to speak quietly.

Affirmation

I allow emotions to reveal meaning gently.

Reflection Question

What emotion feels more resolved now?

Reflection of Choice

Reflection

Reflection is a conscious turning inward.
Today invites you to choose contemplation
without rumination.
Looking back with kindness allows
insight to arise naturally.

Affirmation

I choose reflection with kindness and clarity.

Reflection Question

What memory feels ready to be viewed gently?

Reflection of Rest

Reflection

Understanding does not require effort.
Today invites you to rest in what you already know
without seeking new conclusions.
Rest allows meaning to settle into place.

Affirmation

I rest in understanding without striving.

Reflection Question

What understanding feels complete already?

Reflection in Relationship

Reflection

Winter reflection softens relationships. Today invites you to reflect on connections without needing resolution or change. Understanding alone can bring peace.

Affirmation

I reflect on relationships with compassion.

Reflection Question

What relationship do I see more clearly now?

Reflection in Perception

Reflection

Reflection widens perception.
You may see patterns, themes,
or cycles that were invisible before.
Today invites you to view your experiences
as part of a larger arc.
Perspective creates calm.

Affirmation

I see my life as an unfolding arc.

Reflection Question

What larger pattern is becoming visible?

Reflection in Trust

Reflection

The final act of reflection is trust.
Trusting that learning has occurred
even without conscious effort.
Today invites you to trust what has integrated quietly.
Wisdom does not always announce itself.

Affirmation

I trust what I have learned through living.
Understanding lives within me.

Reflection Question

What learning am I ready to trust without revisiting?

Reflection
Looking back with gentleness and clarity

Embodiment Focus
Witnessing without judgment
Nervous System Tone: Regulation + coherence

Practice

- Sit comfortably with both feet grounded or lie supported
- Allow your spine to lengthen naturally
- Rest your hands in your lap or on your thighs, palms relaxed

1. Settle the breath
- Take a slow inhale through the nose
- Exhale gently through the mouth
- Allow the breath to return to a natural rhythm

2. Create inner distance
- Imagine yourself sitting beside your experiences rather than inside them
- Silently observe:
   - Moments from this season
   - Patterns, efforts, or emotions
- Do not analyze or explain, simply notice

3. Acknowledge without fixing
- Silently complete the phrase:
   "What I see now is…"
- Let the sentence end wherever it naturally does

Remain here for 60–90 seconds, breathing softly.

Why This Supports Reflection

Reflection becomes healing when it is separated from judgment. This embodiment helps the nervous system step out of reactivity and into clarity, allowing insight to emerge without reliving or correcting the past.

*Reflection brings wisdom
when it is met with kindness.*

Nothing hidden, nothing forced.

Acceptance

Meeting what is

Acceptance is not giving up.
it is coming into alignment with reality.

Winter teaches us how to stop arguing with what already exists.
In acceptance, energy is no longer wasted on resistance.
What remains is honesty, steadiness, and peace.

*Nothing needs to be different
for acceptance to begin.*

Acceptance of the Body

Reflection

The body does not need to be corrected
to be worthy of care.
In acceptance, the body is allowed to exist
exactly as it is:
Tired, strong, tender, or changing
without negotiation.

Affirmation

I accept my body as it is today.

Reflection Question

What shifts when I stop trying to improve my body
and simply listen to it?

Acceptance of Emotion

Reflection

Emotions soften when they are allowed.
Acceptance does not ask feelings to disappear;
it asks them to be acknowledged
without resistance or story.

Affirmation

I allow my emotions to exist without judgment.

Reflection Question

Which emotion becomes easier
when I stop trying to change it?

Acceptance of Choice

Reflection

Acceptance releases the pressure to redo the past. Choices made were made with the information, capacity, and awareness available at the time.

Affirmation

I accept the choices that brought me here.

Reflection Question

What would soften if I stopped questioning a past decision?

Acceptance of Rest

Reflection

Rest deepens when it is no longer strategic.
Acceptance allows rest to be enough,
without attaching it to productivity or readiness.

Affirmation

I allow rest without justification.

Reflection Question

What happens when I rest without needing a reason?

Acceptance in Relationship

Reflection

Acceptance in relationship does not mean agreement. it means seeing clearly without needing others to be different in order to feel at peace.

Affirmation

I allow others to be as they are.

Reflection Question

Who might I relate to differently if I released the need to change them?

Acceptance of Perspective

Reflection

Acceptance widens perspective.
When resistance falls away,
reality can be seen without distortion,
urgency, or defense.

Affirmation

I see my life clearly and honestly.

Reflection Question

What truth becomes visible when
I stop resisting what is?

Acceptance of Trust

Reflection

Acceptance is an act of trust.
Trust that life can be met without constant control.
In acceptance, the nervous system rests into reality rather than fighting it.

Affirmation

I trust what is unfolding, even if I do not understand it.

Reflection Question

What would it feel like to trust this moment exactly as it is?

Acceptance

Meeting what is without resistance

Embodiment Focus
Softening into reality
Nervous System Tone: Safety + ease

Practice

- Sit or stand comfortably with your body supported
- Allow your shoulders to relax and your jaw to soften
- Let your hands rest open on your thighs or in your lap

1. Name the moment
- Take a slow inhale through the nose
- On the exhale, silently say:
  - This is what is right now.
- Let the statement land without explanation

2. Soften resistance
- Bring attention to any area of tension in the body
- Without trying to change it, allow the area to soften slightly
- Imagine resistance melting rather than being removed

3. Rest with what remains
- Allow your breath to move naturally
- Stay with the sensation of allowing for 60–90 seconds
When ready, gently return awareness to the room.

Why This Supports Acceptance

Acceptance calms the nervous system by removing the need to fight reality. This embodiment teaches the body that allowing does not mean approving, it means conserving energy and restoring peace.

Acceptance creates space for ease.

Yielding to what is.

Surrender

Letting go of control

Surrender is not weakness.
It is trust without a map.

Winter invites the release of grasping. The softening of plans, expectations, and certainty. In surrender, life is allowed to move without interference.

*You are not being asked to stop caring.
Only to stop forcing.*

Surrender of the Body

Reflection

The body often holds tension
long after effort is no longer needed.
Surrender allows the body to soften its grip
and release what it has been carrying alone.

Affirmation

I allow my body to release what
it no longer needs to hold.

Reflection Question

Where can I let my body soften instead of brace?

Surrender of Emotion

Reflection

Surrender does not mean suppressing emotion.
It means letting feelings move without resistance.
When emotion is allowed to pass through,
it no longer needs to stay stuck.

Affirmation

I allow my emotions to move freely.

Reflection Question

What emotion am I ready to
stop managing or controlling?

Surrender of Choice

Reflection

Not every moment requires a decision. Surrender invites the release of constant choosing and trusts that clarity will arrive when it is needed.

Affirmation

I release the need to decide everything right now.

Reflection Question

What decision can I place down for the moment?

Surrender into Rest

Reflection

Rest deepens when effort falls away.
Surrender allows rest to become restorative
rather than strategic.
A place to land, not a task to complete.

Affirmation

I surrender into rest.

Reflection Question

What happens when I stop trying to rest "correctly"?

Surrender in Relationship

Reflection

Surrender in relationship releases the need
to manage, fix, or anticipate others.
Presence replaces effort,
and connection becomes simpler.

Affirmation

I allow relationships to unfold without control.

Reflection Question

Who or what am I trying to manage
that I could release?

Surrender of Perspective

Reflection

Surrender loosens rigid narratives.
When perspective softens,
reality has room to surprise us
with new understanding.

Affirmation

I release the need to be certain.

Reflection Question

What belief could soften if I allowed not knowing?

Surrender into Trust

Reflection

At its core, surrender is trust embodied. It is the willingness to be held by life without needing proof or reassurance.

Affirmation

I trust what carries me when I let go.

Reflection Question

What supports me when I stop holding everything together?

Surrender
Letting yourself be held

Embodiment Focus
Release of control
Nervous System Tone: Safety + trust

Practice

- Sit or lie down in a position where your body feels fully supported
- Allow your spine, head, and limbs to rest without effort
- Let your hands rest open, palms up or relaxed at your sides

1. Exhale the effort
- Take a slow inhale through the nose
Exhale gently through the mouth, slightly longer than the inhale
- With the exhale, imagine releasing effort downward
- Repeat 2–3 times

2. Allow support
- Bring attention to where your body is being held:
    - Chair
    - Floor
    - Bed
- Silently acknowledge:
    - I am being supported right now.

3. Let go into trust
- Without changing anything, allow your weight to soften further
- Let the breath move naturally
- Remain here for 1–2 minutes, doing nothing else
When ready, gently return awareness to the room.

Why This Supports Surrender

Surrender becomes possible when the nervous system feels safe enough to stop bracing. This embodiment teaches the body that letting go does not lead to collapse.it leads to support, ease, and trust.

Surrender is remembering you are not holding everything alone.

Life enduring through the cold.

Faith

Trusting what cannot yet be seen

Faith is quiet confidence.

Winter strengthens faith by removing evidence. When outcomes are unclear and paths are hidden, trust becomes internal rather than circumstantial.

Faith does not demand proof.
It listens.

Faith of the Body

Reflection

The body has survived countless moments
without instruction or certainty.
Faith lives in the body's quiet intelligence,
the way breath continues, healing happens,
and balance returns on its own.

Affirmation

I trust my body's wisdom.

Reflection Question

What does my body know
how to do without my control?

Faith of Emotion

Reflection

Emotions rise and fall without needing direction.
Faith allows feelings to be experienced
without fear that they will overwhelm or define us.

Affirmation

I trust my emotions to move and pass.

Reflection Question

What emotion am I learning to trust rather than resist?

Faith in Choice

Reflection

Faith softens the need to see the whole path
before taking a step.
It trusts that clarity unfolds through movement,
not certainty.

Affirmation

I trust myself to choose as I go.

Reflection Question

Where have I been supported before,
even without understanding how?

Faith in Rest

Reflection

Rest requires faith.
Faith that nothing will be lost by pausing.
Winter teaches that rest does not delay life;
it restores it.

Affirmation

I trust rest to support me.

Reflection Question

What fear arises when I allow myself to fully rest?

Faith in Relationship

Reflection

Faith in relationship is the willingness to be present without guarantees. It allows connection to exist without control or outcome.

Affirmation

I trust connection to unfold naturally.

Reflection Question

Where can I loosen my grip and allow trust to grow in relationship?

Faith of Perspective

Reflection

Faith widens perspective beyond
what is immediately visible.
It holds the understanding that meaning
often becomes clear only in hindsight.

Affirmation

I trust the larger picture to reveal itself in time.

Reflection Question

What might I understand differently later,
even if I cannot see it now?

Faith of Trust

Reflection

Faith and trust are inseparable.
Faith is the inner knowing that
something meaningful is holding us,
even in uncertainty.

Affirmation

I am supported, even when I do not see how.

Reflection Question

What helps me remember that
I am not alone in this moment?

Faith
Trusting what continues without proof

Embodiment Focus
Inner trust
Nervous System Tone: Safety + steadiness

Practice

- Sit or stand comfortably with both feet grounded
- Allow your spine to lengthen naturally, shoulders soft
- Place one hand over your heart
and one hand over your lower abdomen

1. Anchor in rhythm
- Take a slow inhale through the nose
- Feel the gentle rise beneath your hands
- Exhale softly through the mouth
- Notice the steadiness of breath continuing on its own

2. Notice what persists
- Bring attention to something that continues without effort:
    - Breath
    - Heartbeat
- The support beneath you
- Let this noticing replace the need for certainty
Rest in trust

3. Silently acknowledge:
- Something is holding me, even now.
- Allow the body to settle around this knowing
- Remain here for 1–2 minutes, breathing naturally
When ready, gently return awareness to the room.

Why This Supports Faith

Faith strengthens when the nervous system recognizes continuity and support beyond control. This embodiment helps the body feel trust as a lived experience rather than an idea, allowing steadiness to arise even in uncertainty.

Faith grows where the body feels held.

Beauty without effort.

Grace

Receiving what is freely given

Grace arrives when striving ends.

Winter reveals how much support exists beyond effort: forgiveness, compassion, and mercy that were never withheld, only unnoticed. Grace does not require perfection.

It meets you exactly where you are.

Grace of the Body

Reflection

The body does not ask for perfection to offer healing.
Grace lives in the way the body continues
to breathe, repair, and sustain itself
even when we feel depleted or unsure.

Affirmation

I receive grace in my body.

Reflection Question

Where has my body supported me without being asked?

Grace of Emotion

Reflection

Grace allows emotions to be felt without self-criticism.
It softens the inner voice
and replaces judgment with compassion.

Affirmation

I meet my emotions with kindness.

Reflection Question

What emotion might feel different
if I approached it with gentleness?

Grace in Choice

Reflection

Grace releases the burden of perfect decisions. It understands that growth happens through lived experience, not flawless choice.

Affirmation

I allow myself grace in my decisions.

Reflection Question

What choice can I forgive myself for today?

Grace in Rest

Reflection

Grace allows rest without explanation.
It does not require exhaustion
as proof of worthiness.

Affirmation

I allow rest to be enough.

Reflection Question

What would change if I rested without earning it?

Grace in Relationship

Reflection

Grace in relationship creates space for
imperfection in ourselves and in others.
It softens expectations and deepens connection.

Affirmation

I extend grace in my relationships.

Reflection Question

Who might I relate to differently
if I released unrealistic expectations?

Grace of Perspective

Reflection

Grace widens perspective beyond blame.
It allows life to be seen
with nuance, compassion, and understanding.

Affirmation

I see my life through the lens of grace.

Reflection Question

What story softens when I view it with compassion?

Grace of Trust

Reflection

Grace reminds us that support often arrives quietly
not because we earned it,
but because it exists.

Affirmation

I trust the grace that meets me.

Reflection Question

Where have I been supported without needing to ask?

Grace

Allowing kindness to meet you

Embodiment Focus
Receiving without effort
Nervous System Tone: Safety + softness

Practice

- Sit or lie down comfortably, fully supported
- Allow your shoulders, jaw, and belly to soften
- Let your hands rest open,
palms up or gently placed on your body

1. Open to receive
- Take a slow inhale through the nose
- On the exhale, imagine the body gently opening
 rather than releasing
- Repeat 2–3 times, allowing breath to become effortless

2. Invite kindness
- Silently offer yourself this phrase:
- I do not have to be perfect to be held.
- Notice any softening, warmth, or resistance, all are welcome

3. Rest in allowance
- Let the body remain exactly as it is
- Allow support, warmth, or neutrality to be enough
- Stay here for 1–2 minutes, breathing naturally
When ready, gently bring awareness back to the room.

Why This Supports Grace

Grace is received when the nervous system feels safe enough to stop striving. This embodiment helps the body register kindness, easing self-judgment and allowing compassion to arrive without demand.

Grace arrives when effort rests.

The first movement of return.

Renewal

Restoration from within

Renewal does not begin with action.
It begins with allowance.

Winter restores by replenishing what has been depleted. Energy returns slowly, naturally, without command. Renewal is not something you do, it is something that happens when conditions are right.

Let life refill itself.

Renewal of the Body

Reflection

Renewal in the body does not arrive through effort. It comes through allowing the body time, rest, and gentleness to repair itself in its own way.

Affirmation

I allow my body to restore itself.

Reflection Question

What does my body need in order to renew not improve?

Renewal of Emotion

Reflection

Emotional renewal happens when feelings are allowed to move without being revisited or reworked. Space creates freshness.

Affirmation

I allow my emotions to refresh naturally.

Reflection Question

What emotion feels lighter when I stop holding onto it?

Renewal of Choice

Reflection

Renewal clears old decision patterns.
It creates room to choose differently.
Not because the past was wrong,
but because growth has occurred.

Affirmation

I am open to choosing from a renewed place.

Reflection Question

What choice feels ready to be
approached with fresh eyes?

Renewal through Rest

Reflection

True rest renews more than energy,
it renews clarity, patience, and presence.
In Winter, rest becomes regenerative
rather than preparatory.

Affirmation

I trust rest to renew me.

Reflection Question

What shifts when I allow rest to fully restore me?

Renewal in Relationship

Reflection

Relationships renew when expectations soften. Space, honesty, and presence allow connection to refresh naturally.

Affirmation

I allow relationships to renew in their own time.

Reflection Question

Where might space invite renewal in connection?

Renewal of Perspective

Reflection

Perspective renews when we step out of repetition.
Winter invites us to see life again
without urgency or assumption.

Affirmation

I welcome fresh perspective.

Reflection Question

What feels different when I
look at my life with rested eyes?

Renewal of Trust

Reflection

Renewal restores trust by reminding us that life continues to support us, even after depletion. Trust returns quietly, without announcement.

Affirmation

I trust renewal to arrive gently.

Reflection Question

Where have I been renewed before, without forcing it?

Renewal
Allowing life to restore itself

Embodiment Focus
Gentle restoration
Nervous System Tone: Safety + replenishment

Practice

- Sit or lie down in a position that feels deeply supportive
- Allow your body to be fully held by the surface beneath you
- Place one hand over your heart and
one hand over your lower abdomen

1. Create spacious breath
- Take a slow inhale through the nose
- Exhale gently through the mouth,
slightly longer than the inhale
- Allow the breath to become calm and unhurried

2. Invite renewal
- Silently acknowledge:
- I allow renewal to happen in its own time.
- Let the words land without expectation

3. Notice subtle shifts
- Bring attention to any small sensations of:
  - Warmth
  - Ease
  - Lightness
  - Neutral calm
- Do not search for change, Simply notice what is already present
- Remain here for 1–2 minutes, resting without effort.
When ready, gently return awareness to the room.

Why This Supports Renewal

Renewal does not arrive through effort or intention, it emerges when the nervous system feels safe, supported, and unhurried. This embodiment allows restoration to unfold naturally, honoring Winter's rhythm of quiet replenishment.

Renewal begins when nothing is being asked of you.

Soft, but certain

Hope

The quiet knowing that light returns

Hope in Winter is subtle.

It does not shout or promise certainty. It waits patiently, rooted in the understanding that cycles turn and light always finds its way back.

Hope of the Body

Reflection

The body holds hope in its rhythms.
Breath continues, circulation returns,
and healing unfolds without instruction.
Even in stillness, the body moves toward life.

Affirmation

My body carries hope naturally.

Reflection Question

What small sign of renewal
does my body offer today?

Hope of Emotion

Reflection

Hope in emotion does not deny sadness or grief.
It allows feeling while trusting
that no emotion is permanent.

Affirmation

I trust my emotions to change in time.

Reflection Question

What feeling reminds me that emotions move,
even when they feel heavy?

Hope in Choice

Reflection

Hope loosens the belief
that past choices define the future.
It opens space for new possibilities
to emerge when readiness returns.

Affirmation

I am open to new possibilities.

Reflection Question

What choice feels possible again, even in a small way?

Hope through Rest

Reflection

Rest restores hope by reminding
the nervous system that safety exists.
When the body feels held,
the future feels less threatening.

Affirmation

I allow rest to restore my hope.

Reflection Question

How does rest change my outlook on what is ahead?

Hope in Relationship

Reflection

Hope in relationship allows space for repair, reconnection, and understanding without forcing outcomes.

Affirmation

I trust relationships to evolve.

Reflection Question

Where might patience invite hope in connection?

Hope of Perspective

Reflection

Perspective widens hope.
Winter teaches that cycles turn,
and what feels final is often temporary.

Affirmation

I trust the cycle of change.

Reflection Question

What past season reminds me that
this moment will not last forever?

Hope of Trust

Reflection

Hope deepens trust by anchoring
belief in the continuity of life.
Even when the path is unclear,
movement continues beneath the surface.

Affirmation

I trust that light will return.

Reflection Question

What helps me remember that life
continues to move forward?

Hope
Trusting the return of light

Embodiment Focus
Gentle expectancy
Nervous System Tone: Safety + reassurance

Practice

- Sit or stand comfortably with your body supported
- Let your feet feel grounded beneath you
- Rest your hands lightly over your heart or in your lap

1. Connect to rhythm
- Take a slow inhale through the nose
- Exhale softly through the mouth
- Notice the steady rhythm of breath
continuing without effort

2. Recall continuity
- Silently reflect:
    - I have moved through seasons before.
- Let this remembrance settle into the body
 rather than the mind

3. Hold possibility gently
- Without imagining outcomes,
notice a subtle sense of openness
- Allow this openness to exist without needing direction or speed
- Remain here for 1–2 minutes, breathing naturally
When ready, gently return attention to the room.

Why This Supports Hope

Hope strengthens when the nervous system remembers continuity. This embodiment anchors hope in lived experience — the knowing that cycles turn and light returns
without being forced.

Hope rests in the quiet certainty of return.

Life preparing to rise.

Emergence

The first stirring

Emergence begins before movement.

In Winter, what is new starts internally as a feeling, a knowing, a gentle readiness. Nothing is visible yet, but everything necessary is already present.

Becoming starts long before it is seen.

Emergence of the Body

Reflection

Emergence in the body is often subtle.
A return of warmth, a deeper breath,
a sense of readiness without movement.
The body begins to signal life before action begins.

Affirmation

I notice the quiet signs of readiness in my body.

Reflection Question

What small physical sensation tells me
something is beginning to shift?

Emergence of Emotion

Reflection

Emotional emergence is gentle.
Feelings do not rush forward.
They surface slowly,
asking to be felt rather than acted upon.

Affirmation

I allow emotions to emerge at their own pace.

Reflection Question

What feeling is beginning to make
itself known without urgency?

Emergence of Choice

Reflection

Choice begins as inclination, not decision. Emergence allows options to become visible before commitment is required.

Affirmation

I allow clarity to form before choosing.

Reflection Question

What possibility feels like it is quietly presenting itself?

Emergence through Rest

Reflection

Rest creates the conditions for emergence.
When the body is no longer depleted,
readiness rises naturally.

Affirmation

I trust rest to prepare me.

Reflection Question

What feels more possible when I am rested?

Emergence in Relationship

Reflection

Relational emergence happens when presence returns when connection begins to feel available again without effort or expectation.

Affirmation

I allow connection to reappear naturally.

Reflection Question

Where do I notice a gentle openness toward connection?

Emergence of Perspective

Reflection

Perspective shifts quietly in Winter.
New understanding arrives not through analysis,
but through integration.

Affirmation

I allow insight to rise gently.

Reflection Question

What feels clearer without me
trying to understand it?

Emergence of Trust

Reflection

Trust emerges when the body
senses readiness without fear.
It is the knowing that movement will come
and does not need to be rushed.

Affirmation

I trust what is beginning within me.

Reflection Question

What do I sense is preparing itself to move forward?

Emergence

Noticing the first quiet stirrings

Embodiment Focus
Gentle readiness
Nervous System Tone: Safety + anticipation

Practice

- Sit or stand comfortably with your body supported
- Allow your spine to lengthen naturally, without effort
- Let your hands rest open on your thighs
or lightly over your lower abdomen

1. Sense inward movement
- Take a slow inhale through the nose
- Exhale softly through the mouth
- Bring attention to the space just beneath your breath.
 the subtle feeling of aliveness

2. Notice without naming
- Without searching for answers, notice:
- A feeling of readiness
- A curiosity
- A quiet "yes" or pull toward something undefined
- Let whatever is present be enough

3. Honor timing
- Silently acknowledge:
- Something is beginning, and it does not need to hurry.
- Remain here for 1–2 minutes, breathing naturally
When ready, gently return awareness to the room.

Why This Supports Emergence

Emergence happens when the nervous system feels safe enough to signal readiness. This embodiment helps the body recognize early signs of movement and possibility without forcing clarity or action.

What emerges arrives when it is ready to be seen.

The vastness that holds all things.

Divine Essence

What remains

When roles fall away and seasons pass, something endures.

Winter invites remembrance of what exists beneath identity, achievement, and story. Essence does not change with circumstance. It has always been here.

*This is not something to create.
Only something to remember.*

Divine Essence of the Body

Reflection

Beneath effort, illness, change, and age,
the body carries an intelligence that does not disappear.
Divine essence lives in breath, rhythm,
and the quiet persistence of life itself.

Affirmation

My body carries wisdom beyond
appearance or performance.

Reflection Question

What part of my body feels steady,
even when everything else changes?

Divine Essence of Emotion

Reflection

Emotions move through essence without defining it.
Feelings arise and pass,
but what witnesses them remains unchanged.

Affirmation

I am not my emotions;
I am the awareness that holds them.

Reflection Question

What part of me remains present no matter what I feel?

Divine Essence of Choice

Reflection

Choices shape experience,
but they do not create essence.
Beneath every decision is a deeper presence
that is not altered by right or wrong.

Affirmation

My essence is not determined by my choices.

Reflection Question

Who am I beneath every decision I have made?

Divine Essence of Rest

Reflection

In deep rest, identity softens.
What remains is a quiet sense of being whole,
sufficient, and undisturbed.

Affirmation

I rest in what I am, not in what I do.

Reflection Question

What do I notice when I rest without a role?

Divine Essence in Relationship

Reflection

Essence meets essence in relationship.
Beyond roles and stories, there is a shared presence
that does not need to be managed or earned.

Affirmation

I meet others from the truth of who I am.

Reflection Question

How does connection change when I
stop trying to be someone?

Divine Essence of Perspective

Reflection

Perspective shifts, but essence remains.
When stories fall away, a quiet clarity endures:
steady, compassionate, and unchanged by circumstance.

Affirmation

I trust the truth that remains beneath every story.

Reflection Question

What stays true even as my understanding evolves?

Divine Essence of Trust

Reflection

Trust deepens when we remember that we are held by something greater than effort or certainty. Divine essence does not need proof, it is felt.

Affirmation

I trust the essence that carries me.

Reflection Question

What part of me already knows I am supported?

Divine Essence
Resting in what remains

Embodiment Focus
Being beyond doing
Nervous System Tone: Safety + wholeness

Practice

Sit or lie down in a position where your body feels fully supported
- Allow your eyes to soften or close
- Let your hands rest naturally on your body or beside you

1. Release identity
- Take a slow inhale through the nose
- Exhale gently through the mouth
- With the exhale, imagine setting down roles, names, and expectations

2. Notice what remains
Bring attention to:
- Breath moving on its own
- The quiet awareness that notices sensation
- Do not try to define or understand it

3. Rest as presence
- Allow yourself to simply exist
- No fixing, no becoming, no effort
- Remain here for 1–2 minutes, resting as awareness itself
When ready, gently bring your attention back to the room.

Why This Supports Divine Essence

Divine essence is not created, it is remembered. This embodiment helps the nervous system settle into a state of wholeness beyond identity or effort, allowing presence to be felt rather than conceptualized.

What you are has never been missing.

Nothing missing.

Completion

Honoring what has been lived

Completion is the moment when effort can finally rest.

It is not about closing doors or tying loose ends. It is about acknowledging what has already been carried, felt, and experienced — without needing to revisit, revise, or explain it further.

Winter teaches that completion happens quietly. It arrives when the body exhales, when the heart softens, and when the mind releases the need to keep holding the past open. What has been lived does not disappear; it settles into wisdom.

Completion does not rush what comes next.
It simply blesses what has been.

*Here, nothing more
is required of you.*

Completion of the Body

Reflection

The body completes cycles quietly,
breath finishes its arc, muscles release,
fatigue resolves into rest.
Completion in the body is not dramatic;
it is a settling.

Affirmation

I allow my body to complete what it has carried.

Reflection Question

What does my body feel ready to release or lay down?

Completion of Emotion

Reflection

Emotions complete when they are fully felt
and no longer revisited.
Winter teaches that feelings do not need to linger
once they have been honored.

Affirmation

I allow emotions to complete their movement.

Reflection Question

What feeling feels finished when I stop returning to it?

Completion of Choice

Reflection

Completion does not require certainty about outcomes. It is the moment when a choice no longer needs review, defense, or justification.

Affirmation

I release the need to revisit past choices.

Reflection Question

What decision can I allow to be complete?

Completion through Rest

Reflection

Rest completes what effort began.
In Winter, rest is not preparation.
It is integration, allowing experience to settle fully.

Affirmation

I allow rest to complete this season.

Reflection Question

What shifts when I rest without preparing for what comes next?

Completion in Relationship

Reflection

Completion in relationship does not always mean closure with another person, sometimes it is internal resolution, forgiveness, or peace.

Affirmation

I allow relationships to complete in the way they need too.

Reflection Question

Where do I feel ready to make peace without needing resolution?

Completion of Perspective

Reflection

Completion softens the need to understand everything. Perspective widens when analysis ends a
nd acceptance takes its place.

Affirmation

I release the need to fully understand this season.

Reflection Question

What story no longer needs explanation?

Completion of Trust

Reflection

Trust completes the cycle by allowing what has been lived to stand on its own. Nothing more is required.

Affirmation

I trust that this cycle is complete.

Reflection Question

What am I ready to bless and release?

Completion
Allowing the cycle to settle

Embodiment Focus
Honoring + release
Nervous System Tone: Safety + closure

Practice

- Sit or stand comfortably with both feet grounded
- Allow your shoulders to soften and your breath to slow
- Place one hand over your heart and one hand over your lower abdomen

1. Acknowledge the cycle
- Take a slow inhale through the nose
- On the exhale, silently say:
- This season has been lived.
- Let the words land without analysis

2. Lay it down
- Gently lower your chin slightly toward your chest
- Feel the weight of your hands resting on your body
- Imagine placing down what you no longer need to carry forward

3. Seal with presence
- Lift your head back to neutral
- Take one final slow breath
- Sense the quiet steadiness that remains
- Remain here for 60–90 seconds, breathing naturally.

Why This Supports Completion

Completion allows the nervous system to release unfinished loops. By acknowledging what has been lived and consciously laying it down, the body registers safety, closure, and readiness to rest — without rushing what comes next.

Completion is the moment life exhales.

Winter Closing Ritual

Honoring what has been lived

Winter does not ask for resolution.
It asks for reverence.

This ritual marks the completion of a cycle, not as an ending, but as a moment of acknowledgment. Nothing needs to be fixed, summarized, or prepared. What has been lived is already enough.

Begin

Choose a quiet moment.
Dim the lights or sit near a window.
Bring a blanket, warm drink, or something that feels comforting.

Let this be simple.

1. Settle the Body

Sit or lie down in a comfortable position.
Place one hand over your heart and one over your lower abdomen.

Take three slow breaths:
Inhale through the nose
Exhale gently through the mouth
Allow your body to arrive fully.

2. Honor the Season

Silently or aloud, say:
This season has been lived.
I honor what it asked of me.

Pause.
Let any sensations, emotions, or memories rise
without interpretation.
Nothing needs to be named.

Winter Closing Ritual

3. Acknowledge What Was Carried

Bring to mind:
Efforts you made
Lessons you learned
Emotions you felt
Moments you endured or cherished
Without revisiting the details, simply acknowledge:
This mattered.

Rest here for a few breaths.

4. Lay It Down

On an exhale, imagine gently placing this season down like setting a bundle on the ground.

Silently say:
I do not need to carry this forward.
Notice any softening or release.

5. Seal the Cycle

Return one final breath to your body.
Feel the steadiness beneath you.
Notice what remains when effort ends.

Silently say:
This cycle is complete.
Remain still for a moment longer.

When you are ready, gently re-engage with your surroundings.
There is nothing to do next.
Spring will come in its own time.

What rests will rise.
What has been honored will guide
what comes next.

Cycle Completion

The garden continues

You have reached the end of a cycle
not because something is finished,
but because something has been fully lived.

Like the natural world, your inner life moves in seasons.
There are times to awaken and plant,
times to grow and tend,
times to gather and refine,
and times to rest, remember, and lay things down.

None of these seasons are mistakes.
None of them are permanent.

What you have reflected on here does not belong only to these pages. The questions, the pauses, the moments of clarity and softness, they travel with you.
They will reappear when you least expect them, in new forms,
at new thresholds.

You may return to this book again and again.
You may begin at any season.
You may move slowly, skip pages, or linger where something feels true.

There is no wrong way to tend your inner garden.

Completion is not an ending,
it is a quiet acknowledgment that what needed to be felt has been felt, and what needed to be honored has been honored.

When you are ready,
life will invite you into the next season.
And when it does, you will know how to listen.

Cycle Completion

Before closing the book, pause and ask:

What season am I in right now?

What does this season ask of me gently?

What do I trust will return in time?

The garden within you is never finished.
It is alive and it remembers how to grow.

Author's Note

This book was written as an offering
not to guide you toward answers,
but to remind you that you already know how to listen.

Everything shared here grew from lived experience, reflection,
and reverence for the quiet intelligence
within us all.

If these pages helped you soften, remember, or feel less alone in
your own seasons,
 then they have done what they were meant to do.

May you return to this book
whenever you need steadiness.
May you trust your timing.
May you tend your inner garden
with patience and care.

Thank you for being here
and for honoring your own becoming.

With gratitude,

Amanda E. Robinson

www.ingramcontent.com/pod-product-compliance
Lightning Source LLC
Chambersburg PA
CBHW030100170426
43198CB00009B/437